Reviews

"Terri Simmons has helped me in so many ways. I needed a break with child care because I was going through a tough divorce a few years ago, she gladly gave me a discount for my then 2 year old. When I was fired from my job, she encouraged me to go into day care. She took me through the steps and helped me with my homework. She's wonderful! Buy her book—she knows what she's talking about!"
   MaryJoe Burg, Day Care Provider, Illinois

"I've known Terri for about 6 years personally and what I know of her is that she has a mother's heart for children. She has five of her own and has dedicated her life to those five as well as the many others she continues to care for. She doesn't just do day care because it's convenient, she does it because that is where her heart is; with the children. When it comes to day care, she knows what she is talking about. Take my advice, buy the book!"
   Gayleen Merit, Professional, Illinois

"Terri Simmons has been an encouragement to me in my home day care. She has given me tips on how to plan my day so that it runs smoothly and has also given me information on several programs. I encourage anyone interested in starting a home day care to read this book! Terri is a woman with great wisdom in this area.
   Patricia Donald, Day Care Provider, Illinois

Dedication

To All My Children

michael, marcus, matthew, mitchell, taylor, danial, dantoin, kallani,
jazzman, mikter, asalina, jajuan, laquan, tatianna, cierra, peewee,
chauncey, ryan, winkey, ladaya, nini, wesley, austin, michelle,
maureen, jeramiah, vanessa, brandon, brianna, laragen, jasimine,
joshua, aaron, jc, davonte, ashley, toni, gary, montell, chris, reggie,
porchia, justin, danajia, rashad, ameenah, trevon, quiana, jasmine,
denzel, kianta, dominique, bryce, chrishon, ashley, elisha, and
christopher, who went home to be with the Lord.

Quote

*One hundred years from now, it will not matter what my bank account was,
or the sort of house I lived in, or the kind of car I drove...But the world may
be a little better place because I was important in the life of a child.*

Anonymous

How to Own and Operate Your Home Day Care Business Successfully Without Going Nuts!

**The Day Care Survival Handbook and Guide for
Aspiring Home Day Care Providers and Working Parents**

By Terri Simmons, Ph.D.

First Edition

Amber Books
Los Angeles, CA   Phoenix, AZ

How to Own and Operate Your Home Day Care Business Successfully Without Going Nuts!
by Terri Simmons, Ph. D.

The Day Care Survival Handbook and Guide for Aspiring Home Day Care Providers and Working Parents

Published by: Amber Books, 1334 E. Chandler Boulevard, Suite 5-D67, Phoenix, AZ 85048
E-mail: Amberbk@aol.com

ALL RIGHTS RESERVED

The publication is designed to provide accurate and authoritative information in regard to the subject matter covered. It is sold with the understanding that the publisher is not engaged in rendering legal, accounting, or other professional services. If legal advice or other expert assistance is required, the services of a competent professional person should be sought.

Amber Books are available at special discounts for bulk purchases, sales promotions, fund raising or educational purposes. For details, contact: Special Sales Department, Amber Books, 1334 E. Chandler Boulevard, Suite 5-D67, Phoenix, AZ 85048, USA.

Library of Congress Cataloging-in-Publication Data

Simmons, Terri.
    How to own and operate your own home day care business
successfully without going nuts! : the day care survival handbook
and guide for aspiring home day care providers and working parents /
by Terri Simmons.
      p. cm.
   ISBN 0-9655064-3-6 (alk. paper)
    1. Family day care--United States--Handbooks, manuals, etc.
2. Day care centers--United States--Handbooks, manuals, etc. 3. New
business enterprises--United States--Handbooks, manuals, etc.
4. Home-based businesses--United States--Handbooks, manuals, etc.
I. Title.
HQ778.63.S56   1998
362.71'2'0973--dc21   98-40945
                                         CIP

10 9 8 7 6 5 4
First Printing June, 1999

Contents

Biography

I was in the banking industry for many years. And working away from home and having to leave my children with a sitter was a tough thing to do every day. Not to mention the astronomical Day Care fees that I had to pay out weekly. So, I decided that because my children needed me at home, if at all possible, I would never return to the work place. I became, as many stay-at-home moms do, a "babysitter".

Being a babysitter was not an easy task at first. After spreading the word that I would care for the neighborhood children, I had to figure out what to charge and how to get the parents to pay it. I was sorely disappointed to find that it wasn't as easy at it seemed.

After many, many years of having an unlicensed Home Day Care, My husband and I took the necessary steps to become licensed and were successfully able to release the title of 'babysitter" and declare ourselves as "LICENSED HOME DAY CARE PROVIDERS". And after doing so, we were able to establish a working contract and demand satisfactory weekly payments. In a few short years of becoming licensed, we were able to open CARRIAGE HOUSE, A 24 hr. HOME DAY CARE and BUSINESS CONSULTING SERVICE.

I have owned and operated a Home Day Care for more than 15 years and during this time, I have assisted hundreds across the country in beginning their own Home Businesses through Seminars and Lectures. I was able to write a Manual based on my experiences in Home Day Care, *"The Day Care Survival Manual, A Guide To Helping You Operate Your Home Business Successfully Without Going Nuts!"*, was the basis for this book. The Manual has helped many people in their Day Care ventures and to date, all those who have applied themselves with the knowledge they have gained are very successful.

I was also able to introduce Web Day Care classes on the Internet with interest coming from across the country. I am an instructor in a few local colleges teaching, "The Art of Home Day Care" on weekends. I obtained both my Bachelor's and Master's degrees in Early Childhood Education (1995 and 1997). I then went on to earn my Ph.D. in Early Childhood Education from Hamilton University in Wyoming in February 1999.

My wish is that this new book will reach as well as teach countless individuals, who have a desire to stay at home and make a good living in the wonderful art of Home Day Care. My sole purpose for writing this book is to not only help guide you through the process of operating a Home Day Care but help you to become financially independent from home!

I am confident that after you've completed this book, you'll be able to run your Home Business successfully and perhaps help someone else along the way. My hope is that this book will help you build from my experiences and in return help you to minimize any mistakes.

Remember, there is always money in Child Care because there are so many children who need care. The supply of children never runs out. The cliché is, "If we can do it, anybody can", and it's true. You can make a real good living in Child Care.

Acknowledgments

I have only been able to accomplish this book because of all the little ones who have come into our home and have been a part of our family for more than 15 years. This book is dedicated to you all. I also thank the many parents for trusting me with their little darlings.

First and foremost I give honor to my God, His Son, Jesus, and the Holy Spirit because without whom nothing would be possible in my life.

Second, I give honor to my Pastor, my "Fearless, Spiritual Leader", Apostle Clifford E. Turner, and to his beautiful wife, and my friend, Sister Darlyn Turner. To my wonderful husband, Evangelist Michael W. Simmons, of 19 blessed years. I absolutely adore you. And to our children, Michael Jr., 14, Marcus, 12, Matthew, 10, Mitchell, 8 and our beautiful daughter, Taylor, 3, for sharing your Mommy willingly and without complaining, Thank you!; To my incredibly creative Mom, Ms. Medoria Cheeks for raising me to be true to myself no matter what! Thank you for your love and support, I honor and love you very much.; To my one and only beautiful baby sister, Mrs. Traci Dennard for rejoicing in the little accomplishments with me, Thank you.; And to my Dad and Step-Mom, Mr. and Mrs. Albert and Helen Cheeks for giving me "Cyber-Life" for free! And especially Thank You for being available to me in my countless times of computer hang-ups. Dad, you've really helped me get through the last leg of this project. I love you and again, Thank You so much!

xi

To my magnificently sensitive Elders who have never failed to lend an ear, a shoulder or tissue and who have always encouraged me to stay focused and to trust God-Elder Gloria Thomas, Elder Sharaine Lathon, Elders Autley and Pamela Redwood, Elder Ervin Cross, Elder Charlene Waddell, Elder Maurice Lofton, Elder Ted Colbert, Elder Steven Craig, Elder Lisa McClain, Elder Maxine McCrite, and of course, Mother Gertrude Price, Thank You all for encouraging me.

To Mrs. Bunny Robinson for being the very first to listen to my dreams and visions intensely and with hope. To my wonderful Mother-in-Law, Mrs. Anita Kannedy, my young friend, Nickie Graham and my Spiritual Daughter, SeAndra Steed for being available to coming to my aide quickly and assisting me at a moments notice in Day Care. Thank you. To my sister-in-law, Sharon Hinton, thank you for even going downtown and beginning this whole Day Care process with me. To all of my fabulous friends and family, thank you all. And to all those who inquired on my progress while writing this book and spoke a word of encouragement knowingly and unknowingly. To my Publisher and Editor, Mr. Tony Rose, thank you for being the visionary that you are and for having a worldwide plan for my book. And lastly, to all of my students who have made it a pleasure and a joy to teach about a subject that I love and to the many past, present and future individuals who have learned the art of Home Day Care from my experiences,

Thank you all.

Terri

A special acknowledgment:

    Tony Rose, Publisher and Editor
    Lisa Liddy, Cover and interior design
    Teddy Bear Vothath, Cover photo

As always, the **Publisher** gratefully acknowledges those whose time, patience, help, and advice have contributed to the success of our literary efforts:

Erline Belton; Philip and Anjie Herbert; Felicia Rose and Kate Saylor; Florence Price; Regina Thomas; Elnora Marie Fleetwood-Miles; Yvonne Marie Fleetwood; Kevin Anthony Fleetwood, Jr.; John and Mildred Seagraves; Kay Bourne; Cassandra Latney; Therese Fleetwood; Jamila White; Wayne Summerlin; Lisa Liddy; Rodney J. McKissic; Alfred Fornay; Carolyn Herbert; Tom "Satch" Sanders; Samuel Peabody; Darryl and Lorraine Sanders; Yvonne Rose; the IBBMEC; the Nation's African-American bookstores; our wholesalers and distributors; the black media; and especially Terri Simmons, whose love of God and children everywhere inspired this book.

Foreword

Home Day Care and Child Care Centers are fast becoming the business of the future. While there are definitely pros and cons to any business, Day Care is among the few business there will always be a demand for. In fact, studies show that there aren't enough quality Home Day Care and Child Care Centers to care for the children who are in need of it. Studies also show that the need for more Child Care Providers will press on clear through the year 2000 and beyond.

Today, more than half of the working class women are working mothers with small children 5 years and younger. And the amount of young children with employed mothers are increasing with break-neck speed. But the quality and availability of child care is not keeping up with the demand.

Statistics show that almost 10 million preschoolers were in need of care while mothers worked in 1990 and by 1994 the numbers went well beyond that. Today, the numbers are through the roof. Now more than ever, mothers are returning to work and they are seeking out care for their children in large numbers. Society has changed, stay-at-home-moms, although ideal, are not the norm any more.

Child Care is big business and will get even bigger. Parents are no longer just looking for a "Mom-and-Pop" babysitting operation, they are really looking for an exceptional and stimulating caregiver with more than the traditional "ABC's and 123's" meal. These parents of today will pay top dollar for top-quality care if they can get it. So, if you're planning on opening or currently have a Child Care Service in your area, become aggressive with what you want to offer the children. Studies show that the earlier their little minds are stimulated the more productive they will become as adults. Also, if you are supplying the demand, your clientele will never run dry, your children and their parents will be happy and you'll make some money, maybe not a lot at first, but you'll do okay.

I heard an ex-corporate executive woman once say that she'd rather supervise 100 kids on a daily basis instead of 100 stiff-neck adults any day. "You get to sit on the floor and play with dolls and draw and color!" My sister-in-law who is a Home Day Care Provider once said, "The best part about my Day Care are the hugs and kisses I get every day."

This is not a get-rich-quick business. It takes hard work, time and plenty of patience. Some months you may do well in Day Care, and some months, you'll struggle through those ABC's and 123's. But the demand for care is always there and equally so, the need for finances to enhance the quality of the care that you give is always there as well.

And to help fulfill the demand, the federal government has recently proposed monetary child care packages to not only help facilities across the country enhance the quality of service but to help many low-income families afford child care as well. However, as with anything new, there are correction and adjustments to be made. We who care about the well-being of children must put our "thinking caps" on and come up with ways to improve our centers as these proposals are perfected and implemented throughout the country.

Make no mistake about it, as long as there are children and working parents, there will be a need for child care. Many parents can't rely on relatives to help care for their children, they must come to you, the Day Care Provider, to care for their child.

Terri Simmons, Ph.D.

Introduction

The purpose of this book is to help guide you through the process of beginning a Home Day Care. Caring for several children in your home other than your own twelve hours a day, five days a week is not easy and many mistakes can be made. If this book helps you to minimize them, then I have done my job!

I feel that Day Care is an excellent alternative to finding work outside the home. Especially if you have small children in the home. Instead of being on the paying end of Child Care, which can be astronomical, why not be on the receiving end and make a good living while staying at home.

I'll try my best to point out things like organizational skills, daily scheduling, and simple menu plans that you can incorporate into your own family meal plans. I will of course guide you through the basics of obtaining your license for Day Care, registering your business with your state, working with the USDA Food Program, preparing your home for Day Care, and so much more.

I am confident that after you've completed this book, you'll be able to run your Home Business successfully and perhaps help someone else along the way.

This book is written from my perspective. Every state or county has it's own rules and regulation, therefore I couldn't possibly be specific on *every* point regarding

Home Day Care. I can only give you my experiences with the hope that you can build from them.

I have owned and operated a Home Day Care for more than 15 years and during this time, I have assisted many people in beginning their own Home Businesses. To date those who have applied this knowledge are all very successful in their Day Care ventures. This book was written with the countless other budding Home Day Care Providers such as yourself in mind.

What Do I Do First?

Before you do anything, run out to the store and purchase a note book and pen that's just for you so that you can write all of your thoughts down. Tell your kids to buy their own note pad and pen! This is the beginning for Vision #1 so hands off!

Jot down everything that you like to do concerning Children and Day Care. Make sure that whatever it is, you do it well. Let's say that you like to teach, paint, sew, cook, draw and/or care for children. Look at your list and determine which one can make money first. Decide which one will give you the least amount of resistance, which one needs the smallest amount of capital to get started and hopefully the one you choose will be the same one that brings you the most pleasure.

If you want to start a home day care, you'll definitely need to do a bit of research, ask a lot of questions and go through your local Child Care agency to become licensed as we'll talk about that in a later chapter. Following your Day Care dream won't be exactly a piece of cake, however it will be worth it in the long run. Some of the steps will require more effort than others but you have to decide what amount of effort as well as faith it will take you to accomplish the type of Day Care you want. And when you decide on what you are going to do, you'll be surprised what door will be opened to you just because you took a step of faith in yourself.

True Story:

Years ago I used to publish a magazine on living your dreams. I had my basement set up with a very good computer system. That space was mine and no one was allowed in it. My magazines were moving across the country very well and even in a couple of other countries. Sounds like a winning business. Well it was, but it didn't start out like that.

When I started I had no computer, I had no space available in my basement. I had no background in Advertising or Journalism or even a remote interest in writing professionally. I just wanted to have a mail order magazine that would advertise my arts and crafts. I wanted to make money selling my stuff from home. So I came up with this magazine. I went to the store and purchased a notebook and a good pen just for my business ideas. Not for writing out my grocery list, not for bills. Only for my business. I kept this pad and pen by my bed side at night so that when I'd get an idea in the middle of the night, I could reach over and write it down right then and there.

Weeks went by and I began to write and write. The ideas were developing slowly and I could begin to see my ideas taking shape. It became evident that I now needed a computer. But where was I going to get one. I couldn't take out a loan to purchase a really good one. I was a stay at home mom while my husband worked. He had a good job but his income wasn't nearly enough to support a business and a family too. We were not only struggling hard, we were "*skruggl'in*" to make ends meet. We didn't have little bills, they were so big that we had "Williams!" My husband jokingly remembers, "We had so many bills we had to get approval to pay cash!" Where was I going to get money to put into my business idea. Then I thought, Day Care!

I had been baby-sitting for a couple of children already. The pay was absolutely lousy but none-the-less, I had an avenue I could work with to make the money I needed. I took the necessary steps to become a Licensed Home Day Care Provider so that I could make some real money to put into this business. In the process of doing that, my father called me early one morning and asked if I had a need for a computer. He had one and it was taking up space. If I wanted it I had to come and pick it up immediately! So, I did. In my pajamas and ratty hair, I jumped into my car and flew to his house to get that computer.

I had no knowledge of how to even turn the thing on, let alone operate it. But I was determined to have this business, so I taught myself. It took me about 3 weeks to be able to go from my note pad to my computer. I was able to type out my plan of action. To this day, I don't know what program I was working in or what application I was using. I just know that I got from point A to point B, because I was determined to do so.

I didn't have a background in journalism or advertising. I went to college on an art scholarship. All I knew then was how to draw. But logic took over. I began constructing this magazine based on logic. Obviously I needed advertisements, I needed photographers, I needed a printing company to make this look good, I needed to advertise and most of all, I needed to get my magazine out there to Joe Public!

As I was putting together my thoughts on this craft magazine. Chicago was preparing for it's first "TODAY'S BLACK WOMAN EXPO" at this huge convention center. I live near the city so I discussed with my husband buying a space at this expo, giving out brochures on a magazine that didn't quite exist and selling subscriptions to a magazine that was still just a thought in my head. Now, mind you , I had not a page written. Only a magazine outline, a brochure talking about the purpose of the magazine and an idea of the crafts I was going to put into the magazine. I wanted people to buy my magazine and purchase items like you would any other mail-order magazine.

So, I sent off my $650.00 baby-sitting money to reserve my booth. I had no idea what I was going to do there. I'd had never even been to an expo before so I had no concept of what to expect. I thought I'd need help manning the booth so I mentioned it to my friend Pam who was more than happy to be with me for the 3 days and help me distribute my brochures.

She was a crafter too. She made beautiful Afro-centric lingerie. So I told her to bring her stuff and we'll sell it at the expo. I had a few more friends who heard about my booth and wanted me to sell their stuff too. I really didn't mind because, first of all, I'd get a percentage of their profits plus it would cause people to come into my booth and I would get a chance to talk with them and sell them a subscription.

Man, when I tell you that I had a blast! It was the first time I had stepped out on my faith in business and just "did it"! I had no idea where this was going to go or what was going to happen, but I just did it. And it was fabulous! I spoke with, it seemed, 70 thousand people. My booth was in the perfect spot, near the restaurants. People had to pass me to get to the food stations so I talked with everyone who came past. Because of all of the beautiful craft stuff I had hanging, people flooded my booth.

I should tell you that the booths didn't cost $650.00, they went for $1300.00, so I was actually sharing my spot with a "Fitness Instructor". She was bringing people into her side of the booth and inevitably, they would wander onto my side. I didn't care how they came in. I didn't care that I was sharing my booth. I was just enjoying every second of this expo. And, I didn't sell a thing! Not a cap, not a T-shirt, not a piece of lingerie and certainly not a subscription. Nothing! ***But I had the time of my life***!

I had spoken with dozens and dozens of people who were wearing their talents. They had everything from crafted baseball caps, to painted T-shirts, to jewelry and so on. I encouraged so many people in their talents that it didn't matter that I hadn't sold anything. My natural gift is to encourage, to uplift and motivate. That was what I was doing for 3 solid days, and ***man***, I was having a good time!

Somewhere around the second day, I heard just as clear, "MERGE YOUR MAGAZINE IDEA AND YOUR GIFT TOGETHER". No one said that to me. I wasn't conversing with any one. I was simply staring off into space for one moment and I heard it. I was looking off into the huge crowd of people and I heard it. I was thinking how wonderful it was to be part of an event such as this, and I heard it. Pam was in the isles, talking to people and handing them brochures and I just couldn't get to her fast enough. "Pam, Pam!", I said. "I got it! I got it! I know what I'm going to do with my magazine!"

So, I began putting together my new magazine, *The Money Hunter*. This magazine promised to encourage readers in their gifts and talents. It would showcase other talented black crafters and advertise their crafts for mail-order within each issue. It would feature local black entrepreneurs and how they made it in business. And it would even motivate the reader to go after that dreams.

For me it was an experience that I'll carry for the rest of my life. I stepped out there and did it. Before I knew it, my magazine was in 35 states and 3 countries before it's final issue. Due to medical reasons, I had to close production of *THE MONEY HUNTER*. But that was an experience among many that I'll share with you.

As you go through this business adventure, you'll have magnificent experiences, as well as overwhelming disappointments; but, the key is to keep going. You have to do something towards your dream *Every Day*.

Keep at it no matter what. You have to keep going or it will die. Trust yourself. You're on the right track if you have faith in yourself. You have to know that you will not fail! Sure, you'll fall down and even make a huge mess of things some time along the way but you will not fail because every mistake is a chance to begin again, more intelligently! If you learn from your mistakes, it was a lesson and not a failure. If you learn from it, you'll not make the same mistake again. ***But a lesson unlearned is a lesson returned***.

Learn from each event in your business adventure. Don't give up because you think it's to difficult or too time consuming. Time is going to pass anyway so you might as well work towards what you love while it passes!

Most of all, don't share your dream with just any body. There are vision killers in your life. There are people all around you who do not want you to succeed. They are your parents, your best friends, your sisters and brothers and even your spouse. Many times they don't mean to kill your vision, they just don't see what you see. They don't want you to get hurt and waste time, energy and money on a "kooky" idea. As much as you want to share your ideas with people, know who to share it with and at what time.

And Heaven forbid you share it before you have confidence in it yourself and in what your really want to do. Some things you just don't talk about before it's done. Because you are going to come up against opposition, you have to first get your head straight and your vision in focus before you try to gain approval from someone else. People will disappoint you and have you doubting yourself, if you are not careful. Don't look for the approval. If you get it great. However, you may not get it at all.

You must have faith in the God who created you, faith in your self and faith in your vision. If you are looking for other people to approve of your idea, you'll be disappointed every time. Don't be afraid of what other people might say about your vision, your dream, YOUR BABY. It's yours already and they cannot take it from you. The God of all Glory has given you this dream to go and fulfill it to the best of your ability so don't let anyone intimidate you. If you know down in your "gut" that this is what you are going to do, don't be ashamed of it. Even if everything isn't quite in place yet. If you have mega confidence in it, who cares if it's still a dream. The point is that your gut will birth it into reality!

When you are asked about your business, hold your head up and square your shoulders; and with confidence tell them all about it, that is if you have it all put together in your head to tell them. Don't give anyone a reason to call you shaky because you are unsure of yourself.

The bottom line is, trust yourself and don't be afraid. You can do absolutely nothing unless you run right at your fears. Stop being afraid to stick your neck out there. How do you know what's going to happen? Use the common sense that God has given you and trust HIM, trust yourself and begin to build and move toward your vision.

Great people didn't just become great. They made great mistakes along the way. Mistakes are simply a chance to begin again more intelligently. That's why erasers are on pencils, everyone makes mistakes. If you do nothing but make mistakes for the first few years, your are not only doing something wrong, but you are also learning what not to do again. It also shows that you are trying. For nothing beats a failure but a try. People who try hard at nothing succeed every time. In other words, if you don't try, you get no where really fast.

It takes time, planning and guts. Write our your plan. You've heard it said that if you fail to plan, you plan to fail. And that seems to be the make up of many failed businesses. They had a fabulous idea but they didn't write it out plainly enough. They didn't research it out well enough and they surely didn't have the guts to walk it out long enough. Without guts you can't get very far. It takes courage to do anything worth while. You may be asking yourself, how can you get guts. Can you purchase a bottle of it? Well, you really don't have to go anywhere to get it. You have it already. Courage is already inside each of us who dares to dream at all. Courage is faith in yourself, faith in your God and faith in your dream. Faith is simply belief. If you can believe in it, it's already done. All it takes is walking it out step by step. Even before you see it come to pass, if you believe in it, it's already accomplished.

Don't be afraid of your dream. Run at that fear. My Pastor, who is a Great Man of God, has said many times that fear is only "False Evidence Appearing Real". Don't let fear stop you from doing any great thing. You'll never see how great you really are if you stop every time you are afraid. You'll never discover the greatness inside you if you don't begin to take great steps. Great people make great mistakes. Great buildings have great foundations and great dreamers have great successes.

Get a vision of yourself doing that dream. Seek God and ask HIM to clarify that vision. Ask HIM to help you understand every inch of that dream so you'll know exactly what you're to do next. Write everything down and ask many, many questions. Seek out people who have done similar things that you desire to do and ask them for advice. If they don't seem to want to be an encouragement to you, skip on and go to your next source of information. God has fixed it so that there are people stationed at every step of your success ladder to help you up. And every step must be thought out carefully so that you don't slip. Oh, you may miss a step here and there and you may even slip for a moment; but get back up and continue on. One thing is for sure, if you **do** keep going, you have no choice but to **get there**!

What is the Second Thing I Must Do?

Now that you have your note pad and you've jotted things down and you've put them in order according to what you want to do first, let's start at the top. Let's say you have now decided to start a Day Care.

You certainly have to come up with a name. So throw the names around. Make sure that it says what you do. Don't call your Day Care, "Debbie's". What does that say? Who is Debbie and what does she do? Now if you say something like, "Debbie's Kiddie Care at Home" or "Tot Ville, U.S.A.", you're telling people you care for children in the home. If you say, "Lu-Lu's," what is a "Lu-Lu's? But if you say, "Lu-Lu's Day Care Center," people will know who you are.

So, we have Lu-Lu's Day Care Center. Now what? Well, you have to call your state's county clerk's office and ask them for the number to your local Small Business Association. We'll go into a little more detail in a later chapter, but remember that every Association is different so you'll have to find out what is your next step according to your states requirements for registering and filing your business.

Lu-Lu's Day Care has now been filed with the state as a legitimate service. But now you must be licensed; and your chosen facility must be licensed and inspected to care for children. Will you be a Home Day Care or a Day Care Center? You have to decide. They are two totally separate businesses with completely separate rules and regulations set forth by your local states government. So search it out. Call your local Department of Children and Family Services and find out about their Orientations Classes. Go to both and find out which one will suite you better. A Home Day Care may not require any special college courses, however, you will have to sacrifice a portion of your home for the children. A Center has far more requirements but your home isn't involved and you can have many more children and make much more money than you would from a Home Day Care. You have to make a decision and stick with it. Go to the orientations so that you'll be making the best possible decision based on the information received. It's not going to be effortless, however. Once you have reached your goal, you will have a huge sense of accomplishment. Anything you choose, if you want it bad enough, you'll do what it takes to make it happen.

If you are going to go into a day care business, you must have some knowledge in caring for children. Disaster is waiting for you if you're entering into a business that you have no background in. So, please make sure you know your stuff before you declare yourself in business.

Do your research, perfect your craft, learn your stuff so that you can give the best possible service. And ultimately, one door will lead to another door. Today it may be Home Day Care, but tomorrow it may be a String of Day Care Centers around the country. Opportunities are just out there sitting and waiting for you. Ideas come from active minds. When you are working on Plan A, Plan B is right there ready to fall in line.

Your talents will multiply, just like rabbits! You'll have one, then another and another and another. And that's what is so marvelous about believing in yourself. When you trust yourself, you know each talent, idea or gift that you have is possible.

God gives each of us a measure of talent, or idea #1, which will grow into idea #2 and so on. Any hamburger joint that you see on the street also sells chicken and fish patties. Why? Because idea #1 went into idea #2 and #3. ***You talents will multiply if you just get the first one started.***

You must understand that if you make use of a gift or idea that God has given to you, HE will multiply your ideas. Just like money in the bank, if you invest $100.00 wisely, you'll get more than what you started out with, but if you take that same $100.00 and stick it in a drawer because you don't want anyone to steal it, it can never do anything for you. It will never grow and you will never get a return on it.

Trust yourself. How do you know what Day Care will lead to if you don't get started? Trust yourself, trust your instincts and just go for it. And while you are on the right track don't stop. You can be on the right track but if you stop, you'll get run over by a train! Keep going and never stop.

Keep Going!

Let's Be Serious For A Moment…

How many times are you confronted with the question. "So, what do you do?" And you stumble with the simple answer…"I'm in business for myself…" Is it that you don't quite have a vision in focus? Or is it that you don't have confidence in the vision that you do have?

When asked about your occupation do you begrudgingly say, "Oh, I'm just a home-maker," instead of saying "Yes, I'm a Domestic Engineer and a darn good one, too!", or "I work for the school system" when you really should be saying, "Oh, Honey, I'm the best Doggone 4th Grade Teacher at West Dale Elementary!". But you don't say that either. Your heart's desire is to **design your own line of clothing for your own store** but you don't dare say that because you're not sure of yourself and you probably can't pull it off. Or what your really want to do in life is own a thriving **Home Day Care** and eventually have a string of **Day Care Centers across the country**, but you can't convince yourself to even take the first Day Care class at the local college.

Heaven forbid you should speak on that **Million Selling Novel** that you've been secretly working on. Are you secretly thinking that perhaps you're not good enough or even capable of coming up with such a marvelous ideal. Might you be wondering who would be interested in a book written by someone such as yourself. Your life is boring and your talents are virtually non-existent! Could you be saying to yourself that your dreams are far too ridiculous to even speak out loud. **Says Who!!**

Chapter 1
The Paperwork

The Paperwork

Now that you've established that this is really what you want to do you have to lay your foundation for it. Now, no one says that you have to do this for the next 15 years. Perhaps, you just want to do this for a few years to put your children through school, pay off a few bills, meet a few goals or simply to come off your job so that you can be your own boss.

You may just love this career enough to do it some 20 years or more. However long you operate your business, make sure the time and effort you put into your business is worth it. It's crazy to do all of the paperwork involved and acquire the children only to quit in 6 months. If you do this, make it worthwhile not only to yourself, but to the children and parents concerned.

Now, for the foundation

What you want to do is call your **Department of Children and Family Services** in your state or county, asking them to send you information on becoming a **LICENSED HOME DAY CARE PROVIDER**. Be sure to ask them to send you information on their orientation, with dates and times and anything else pertaining to licensing.

Once that information comes in the mail, read it carefully. Fill everything out and mail it promptly. (Example A) Go to the orientation, if there is one, and you may not have to, but, be prepared to stay for most of the day. Take a lunch or plenty of change for the vending machines. (Please remember that all examples are for you to have some idea of what your forms may look like. No form in this book is official or exact.)

The orientation class is for potential Day Care Providers, taught probably by DCFS Licensing Representatives. They discuss not all, but many areas of Day Care and will answer most of your questions. It may be all day; and at the end of the class, they will give you a packet which includes a listing of what you'll need for Day Care: how you should prepare your home, a list of Food Program Providers in and around your area, Application for Family Home Licensing forms, (example B), Background check forms, (Example C), Adult Medical Record forms, (example D), (Your local DCFS will give you children medical record forms or you can simply get them from your doctor), a copy of the licensing standards and procedures and other forms that MUST be filled out completely and returned. Remember, your states' procedures may be different

OR…You can shop around and look for a local Human Development Center in your area. Not all states have this assistance readily available so you may have to dig to find one.

If you do locate one, call and ask about their process and if it suits your needs, go through their process. Hopefully they will be able to instruct you in the area of Home Day Care with no problems.

They can be much more thorough because many of these agencies are designed to work individually with you, (in your home if necessary) to bring you up to your state's standards.

Their classes may run anywhere from 4 to 9 weeks and will probably go through most areas of Day Care. Subjects should range from setting up your home, to contracts, to filling out menus and so on. Somewhere during the weeks of class, a DCFS Representative might attend and discuss briefly some of the things that are discussed at length during orientation and you might even be able to pick up the same packet that you would at the DCFS orientation. These classes are very helpful. They are fun and very informative, and can help you with creativity in your day with the children. However, they may not be mandatory. You have to check with your state. They are designed to give you added support and confidence as you begin your Day Care.

BUT…You may not have to do that either. If you have a working knowledge of children because of your past experiences, you may not have to take these classes at all. And contrary to popular belief, **in some states you do not need college courses or a degree to run a home Day Care.** You may be able to go to the one time orientation and call it a day! Send in the information from the packet and call DCFS when you think you are ready for your home inspection. Remember, you have forms and things that need to be done.

The forms may include but probably are not limited to:

❑ **MEDICAL RECORD FORMS** for you and every member of your family.

❑ **BACKGROUND FORMS** for every one in your home usually over the age of 13.

❑ **FINGER PRINTING** for every one in your home usually 18 years and over.

❑ The finger printing may or may not be a form, but you must have it done. Inquire at your local Police Dept.

❑ **CPR & INFANT FIRST AIDE** You must know this and have a certificate. Inquire at your local Fire Department or Red Cross. It doesn't cost much.

Every adult in the home is licensed because at some point they may have to care for the children and they must be cleared by DCFS.

AND DON'T THINK you'll be able to get around any of these important forms! You may get around it today but tomorrow they WILL catch up with you.

Let's say you put in false information about the amount of adults in your home. You, for instance, won't put your brother, Bill's name down because he just got out of prison and he'll be moving out in a few short weeks. So you send in all of the information minus your brothers name. While your brother is away meeting with his Parole Officer, you schedule your Representative to come out. Everything goes well and your house clears inspection for Day Care.

You receive your license in the mail. Your Day Care clientele includes excellent paying parents who are very generous and who bring their children every day. Your Day Care is going along smoothly and you think that you've beaten DCFS.

Brother Bill, who has not moved yet, is in the basement watching re-runs of "I Love Lucy" and your son's school calls to tell you that he's been in a fight and you must come immediately! No one else is available and you MUST go. Brother Bill is on "House Arrest" so he can't leave the premises except by permission from his Parole Officer. He must stay and watch the Day Care children. While you are out, one of your most generous parents have come early to pick up their child and brother Bill answers the door.

You can say, "Oh, that will never happen to me, I don't have a brother Bill." But you may have some secret thing that if DCFS knew about it, it could cost you your license. Of course everyone has skeletons in their closet, but what I'm telling you is: "Do the very best to be accurate and honest with your information concerning Day Care." You don't want it to come back and haunt you later.

Also, the way *you* think isn't necessarily how the rest of the world thinks, particularly your Day Care parents. And in the situation I've just mentioned, you might think they'd understand; but look at it from their point of view. A strange man, whom they know nothing about, is just out of prison and is watching their child. You never told anyone about him. And you definitely did not have their permission to leave their child with anyone else, especially an EX-CON!

You never want to leave yourself open to be publicly embarrassed or potentially sued because you tried to cover up something that directly affects your Day Care.

True Story:

I had a friend named Alice some years back who was a Provider. While her Day Care was going along quite well, she became pregnant and had some sudden complications which caused immediate bed rest for the duration of her pregnancy. She couldn't stop the Day Care because she needed the money but she couldn't run it either. So she had to hire a full time assistant to run it for her. She hired her friend JoAnna. She was a wonderful West African woman whom she fully trusted to be in her home some 12 to 15 hours every day. She was excellent! She not only ran her Day Care but she cooked 3 meals every day and cleaned too!

After a few days, Alice asked JoAnna to please fill out the necessary forms because she must be licensed as well. JoAnna took the forms and went back to her work. About a week went by and the forms still were not done. Alice noticed JoAnna began to make excuses as to why these forms could not be filled out. Finally, Alice asked her for the real reason. JoAnna confessed that she was an illegal alien. She had come to the U.S. for a visit and looked up one day and it was 14 years later. She had kept this part of her life a complete secret. She'd been here all that time without becoming a citizen of the U.S. and her time had been up 6 months after she had arrived.

Alice simply asked her to call a lawyer and fix the problem. She could not, because not only had she broken the law here in the U.S., but she had broken the law in her country as well. To go back or even to try to gain citizenship here would mean certain imprisonment for many, many years. And she had her own children to think about.

As much as she trusted JoAnna in her home, as much as she needed her services, she couldn't have her there. If something were to have seriously happened to one of Alice's Day Care children and she knew of her assistant's personal situation, she stood a chance of being investigated, shut down and/or sued. All of the parents knew JoAnna and they really loved her but it was an impossible situation to keep up. As painful as it was, Alice had to let her go. She was able to work things through concerning her pregnancy and Day Care and had a healthy baby girl.

If you're in a situation that DCFS cannot approve of, do your very best to rectify it or find another way to use your Home Day Care Services.

I have a friend who cannot do Home Day Care because her husband has made some really bad boo-boo's in his past, however, she shares her teaching background with other Home Day Care Providers by coming into their homes once or twice a week for a couple of hours and teaching pre-school "stuff" to the children.

She was able to be approved of, but her husband was not. So she is still on her own time, being her own boss, and making money her way.

REMEMBER, this is your business and you want to maintain a professional attitude with it. This is one you want to be proud of. Don't do anything that will cause you to hang your head in shame. It's awfully hard to live bad choices down. When you mess up with other peoples' children, you are forever chained to it. Like the famous Black film director, Spike Lee said, *"DO THE RIGHT THING!"*

Family Home Information

This form is used to give a general picture of your family, stability, home and income.

IL 418-506
Rev. 12/83

State of Illinois
Department of Children and Family Services

FAMILY HOME INFORMATION

PLEASE CHECK THE TYPE OF LICENSE FOR WHICH YOU HAVE MADE APPLICATION

Foster Family Home   Day Care Home

I.   NAME: Applicant A _____
                           (Last)   (First)   (Middle)

            Applicant B _____
                           (Last)   (First)   Middle

    ADDRESS _____
                 (Street or Rural Route)

            (City)   Zip Code   (County)   (Telephone)

    How long have you been a resident of Illinois? Applicant A: ____ (Months) (Years)   Applicant B: ____ (Months) (Years)

II.   HOME—Check any boxes that apply

    DO YOU ☐ OWN ☐ RENT   LANDLORD APPROVAL TO CARE FOR UNRELATED CHILDREN ☐ Yes ☐ No
             ☐ APARTMENT   ☐ MOBILE HOME ☐ HOUSE ☐ OTHER

    WATER SUPPLY ☐ CITY ☐ OTHER (Specify) _____

    DIRECTIONS FOR REACHING YOUR HOME _____

III. MARITAL STATUS—Check One Box

    ☐ MARRIED _____
                     (Date)
    ☐ SINGLE ☐ WIDOWED
    ☐ DIVORCED ☐ LEGALLY SEPARATED

PREVIOUS MARRIAGE: CHECK IF YES
☐ APPLICANT A   ☐ APPLICANT B

IV. MEMBERS OF HOUSEHOLD
    (Include Children, Relatives, Others)

NAME	RELATIONSHIP	BIRTHDATE	LANGUAGES SPOKEN	RELIGION
Applicant A:				
Applicant B:				

V. CURRENT EMPLOYMENT

	Name of Firm	Address	Title or Position	Working Hours	Years Employed
Applicant A				___ to ___	
Applicant B				___ to ___	

APPROXIMATE ANNUAL INCOME OF TOTAL HOUSEHOLD, REGARDLESS OF SOURCE _____

24

CFS 597A
IL 418-0019
Rev. 7/95

State of Illinois
Department of Children and Family Services
APPLICATION FOR FAMILY HOME LICENSE

Complete in duplicate.
Retain one copy for your file.

DO NOT WRITE IN THIS SPACE—AGENCY USE ONLY

Region/Site/Field
Responsible for License _____

Date Received _____

Date Entered _____

County No. _____

Supervising Agency No. _____

For DCFS Use Only.
☐ Independent Home

☐ DCFS Regional Office
☐ Licensed Child Welfare Agency
☐ Licensed Day Care Agency
☐ Licensed Exempt Agency

Name _____
Street Address _____
City _____ Zip _____
Telephone No. _____

Field Office _____

PLEASE READ INSTRUCTIONS ON THE BACK BEFORE COMPLETING THIS APPLICATION

APPLICATION FOR (Check One)   ☑ INITIAL LICENSE   ☐ RENEWAL OF LICENSE Number _____

APPLICANT PLEASE CHECK THE TYPE OF LICENSE FOR WHICH YOU ARE APPLYING
(Check One Only)

☐ Foster Family Home   ☑ Day Care Home   ☐ Group Day Care Home

Name of Applicants: A. _____
Last Name   First   Middle

☐☐☐-☐☐-☐☐☐☐ Social Security No.

B. _____
Last Name   First   Middle

☐☐☐-☐☐-☐☐☐☐ Social Security No.

Address _____
No. and Street   City and Zip   County

Mailing Address _____
No. and Street   City and Zip   County

Home Telephone _____   Work Telephone _____
Area Code   Number   Area Code   Number

ALL APPLICANTS PLEASE ANSWER THE QUESTIONS BELOW AND SIGN THE APPLICATION

1. The Department frequently receives requests from businesses, organizations and local government jurisdictions for lists of family home licensees. If you wish to have your name excluded from these listings, check (✓) here: ☐
2. Have you ever been convicted for other than a minor traffic violation?   ☐ No ☐ Yes
   If yes, explain:
3. Are you currently licensed for child care in Illinois? ☐ No   ☐ Yes License No(s). _____
   If yes, give type of license(s) _____
   Name on license(s) _____
   Address on license(s) _____
4. Have you ever been licensed for child care outside Illinois? ☐ No   ☐ Yes License No(s). _____
   If yes, give type of license(s) _____
   Name on license(s) _____
   Address on license(s) _____
5. If you are not currently licensed for child care, complete the questions below:
   Have you ever applied for a child care license? ☐ No   ☐ Yes
   Was license issued? ☐ No ☐ Yes
   If yes, give type of license _____
   Name on license _____
   Address on license _____

I(WE), the undersigned, representing the facility herein named, hereby apply for license to operate a child care facility under the Child Care Act of 1969 as amended. I (WE) declare that, I (WE):
I.   Have received a copy of the standards, have read and are familiar with the standards for which license is sought.
II.   Will be subject to investigation upon application in regard to meeting standards
III. Will cooperate with the licensing agency through the study.
IV.   Are aware that to operate a child care facility without a license or permit constitutes a Class A misdemeanor and that I (WE) may be prosecuted for such misconduct.
V.   Will be subject to supervision in terms of conformance with minimum standards upon issuance of a license.
VI.   Affirm that the information provided above is true. I (WE) understand that making materially false statements in order to obtain a license or permit constitutes a Class A misdemeanor and that I (WE) may be prosecuted for such misconduct.

Application For Family Home License

This is an application which gives the Licensing Representative an idea of what kind of license you desire. And your history of previous licenses, if any.

Authorization For Background Check

This form, if filled out honestly, gives the Licensing Representatives a general picture into your character. It gives them permission to check into your past for any adverse activity that they may consider unsafe for the children that you may serve.

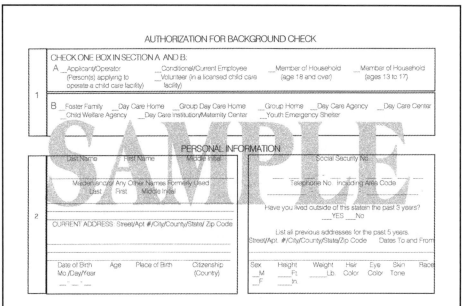

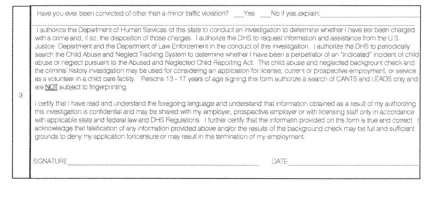

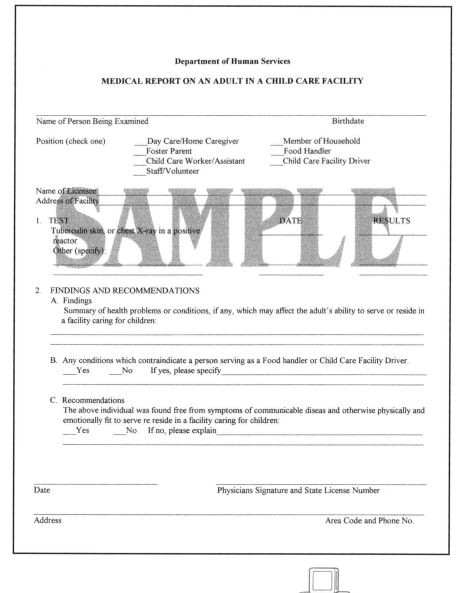

Department of Human Services

MEDICAL REPORT ON AN ADULT IN A CHILD CARE FACILITY

Name of Person Being Examined   Birthdate

Position (check one)   ___Day Care/Home Caregiver   ___Member of Household
                            ___Foster Parent   ___Food Handler
                            ___Child Care Worker/Assistant   ___Child Care Facility Driver
                            ___Staff/Volunteer

Name of Licensee
Address of Facility

1. TEST   DATE   RESULTS
    Tuberculin skin, or chest X-ray in a positive
    reactor
    Other (specify):

2. FINDINGS AND RECOMMENDATIONS
    A. Findings
        Summary of health problems or conditions, if any, which may affect the adult's ability to serve or reside in
        a facility caring for children:

    B. Any conditions which contraindicate a person serving as a Food handler or Child Care Facility Driver.
        ___Yes   ___No   If yes, please specify

    C. Recommendations
        The above individual was found free from symptoms of communicable diseas and otherwise physically and
        emotionally fit to serve re reside in a facility caring for children:
        ___Yes   ___No   If no, please explain

Date   Physicians Signature and State License Number

Address   Area Code and Phone No.

Medical Record Form

This is a form for your Physician to complete that explains your general health. It tells the Representative that you are free from any communicable diseases and whether or not you are physically able to care for children.

27

Chapter 2
Inspections

Inspection

Now, before you can call your Representative for an inspection appointment, you have to prepare your house or apartment. Yes, I said apartment. You can have your Day Care in an apartment. If that's where you live, and you have approval from the Landlord, then you can have it there. Check with your states DCFS before you begin. This business is called a HOME DAY CARE. If you happen to live in an apartment, don't count your Day Care vision as a loss before you even check it out. Wherever your home is, assuming it is a legal and safe dwelling, that is where you can have it.

You must prepare your home by first establishing where you will have the children for most of the day. Let's assume you will have them in the living room of your home.

❑ 1. The floor should be smooth and clear of chipping floor planks or carpeted.

❑ 2. You need to have all of the outlets covered.

❑ 3. Any dangling cords must be bound up and out of reach of children or protected so that they cannot get to them.

❑ 4. Your TV and VCR must be protected from the children.

❑ 5. You need to have gates to confine the children to one room and keep them from the stairs at all times.

❑ 6. Put door knob covers on all doors that you don't want the children opening.

❑ 7. If you have a fireplace, you can purchase protection corners for the stone base. And you must have a promissory letter stating that you will not use the fireplace when Day Care children are present or during Day Care hours.

And in general, crawl around and look at your living room at a child's eye level. Children are smarter than we ever give them credit for, so remove anything that even has the potential of harming a child.

Let's move to the kitchen. You of course will be preparing and probably feeding the little ones in the kitchen.

❑ 8. The floor tiles must be smooth and flat, free of chips, and missing tiles.

❑ 9. The cabinets must all either be secured with child safety locks or emptied of anything that is potentially poisonous and/or dangerous.

❑ 10. All cleaning supplies must be out of reach of children or securely locked away.

❑ 11. If you have an older model stove, you need to purchase stove knob covers to prevent children from turning on the stove. The newer model stoves take some coordination to turn on. And you must have a working smoke detector on every level of your home.

Okay, let's go over this again. Your Licensing Representative will be looking for the aforementioned items, as well as a few more pieces of information listed below. Having all of these things will make your visit run much more smoothly for inspection.

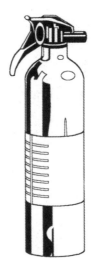

❑ A medical form for each member of your household must be available at the time of the visit.

❑ A charged "ABC" fire extinguisher in your kitchen(s)

❑ A working smoke detector on each floor level (whether used for Day Care or not).

❑ A first Aide supply kit—including Band-Aids, tape, sterile gauze pads, tweezers, and mild soap.

❑ Protective covers in all unused electrical outlets that are accessible to the children.

❑ Protective barriers around heating sources.

❑ Copies or documents showing that your pet's inoculations are up to date.

❑ A written emergency evacuation plan with a drawing that shows all exits.

❑ Automobile insurance document in case of field trips for the Day Care children. (Always get the parents' written permission to take the children out on trips. You must also have enough room to safely transport the children to and from.)

❏ A federally approved Car Seat for each child riding in your automobile. **(Please remember that if you do have a vehicle that has a passenger-side air bag, any child under 12 years should not ride in the passenger seat, even if they are in a child safety seat. children have been killed or seriously injured by the deployment of the air bag.)**

❏ Home or Renters insurance covering individuals in case of a serious accident in your home.

❏ Sufficient beds, cots, cribs and/or playpens for napping.

❏ A mobile or bright hanging toy for over the sleeping spaces of young infants.

❏ A toddler potty chair for each training toddler.

❏ A sufficient amount of toys suitable for the ages of the children that you care for.

❏ MUST have a CPR and Infant First Aide Certification, (Call your Fire Dept. for information.)

(Your state may require more then these listed items.)

I would say you may spend between $40.00 and $100.00 on safety supplies. It depends on the size of your home and where you shop. Some things you may be able to get around like screwing locks into your cabinets. If you'd rather not do that

to keep the children out, simply empty the lower cabinet and move the dangerous items to an upper cabinet.

Cabinets are very expensive and you may not want to put holes into your cabinet doors. If you don't already have handles for the handle type locks and can't screw the holes in, just move the items out of danger.

You can use your bedrooms if you wish, however, you must have separate sheets and pillows for the children to sleep on. You have to have enough sleeping space for the amount of children that you have. The bedrooms must be safe as well if you are going to use them for Day Care. The same precautions apply. Look around and correct each bedroom for inspection.

Also, the bathrooms must be inspected. You must remove those items from under the sink unless you are going to put locks on the cabinets. You may want to put door knob covers on the bathroom doors to keep them from entering without your knowledge.

You must have a sterile solution like bleach and water in a spray bottle to clean and disinfect areas after diaper change or accidents on furniture or play equipment. It's one part bleach to 3 parts water. You should always have that on hand as accidents happen ALL the time.

True Story:

I can remember several years ago, I was caring for two brothers, Larry and Robert. The younger one, Larry, was very content to sit quietly all day playing with toys. The other, Robert, was very vocal. He would follow me around the house all day asking question after question. He was huge. When I say huge, I mean he could wear my 12 year old son's size 14 shirts and he was only 3 years old! To be so big, HE WAS NOT POTTY TRAINED AT ALL!

We had purchased a big plastic jungle slide for them to play and climb on while in the house. Every day, his mother would insist that he is trained and I should have no problems. She would put regular pants on him, drop him off and go. And every day, I was spraying and disinfecting that jungle slide with my bleach solution. He would tell me everything except that he had to use the bathroom. Instead, he'd use it on the slide.

At the end of each day, I'd tell her that he is not ready for regular pants and it made my day harder because I had to spend most of the time cleaning up after his really nasty messes. It seemed that she just never got what I was saying. I found out later that she understood perfectly. The reason she pretended to play "dumb" was because she just didn't want to purchase the Adult size diapers that were needed for him!

Her home was seriously disturbed. She had a job and was on Public Aide. However, she was incredibly poverty stricken not only in the pocket, but in the mind as well. Diapers for the older child were not a necessity for her. After about 5 months, she and I couldn't see eye to eye so I asked her not to bring them back.

You may want to keep on hand extra wash cloths for Day Care. Not to say that you won't need baby wipes but you may need to dish out a bath or two during the week. Whenever possible buy in bulk. Register at a local club warehouse and do your bulk shopping. You'll run out faster and end up spending more if you shop at regular stores.

Let's Talk Furniture & Toys!

Somewhere on your list of frustrations and anxieties you're haggling over where to purchase ALL of this baby furniture that you will need for your Day Care. Rest easy, everyone and I do mean everyone has an Uncle Jack or a cousin Martha who has stored their old baby furniture in the back of the garage, attic or basement. All you have to do is just get the word out to your friends and relatives that you are starting a Day Care and are on the look out for baby furniture.

They may not want to give these things up without a fight, so offer them a small pittance for these items. And if you don't have it available now, give them an honest I OWE YOU ticket, and then pay them that $25 or $30 dollars after you've gotten paid from your first month. After a while, the word will spread and before you know it you will have collected all that you need.

The other thing you can do is call other larger Day Care facilities in the yellow pages and ask them if they have used Day Care furniture stored away that they'd be willing to sell for a small fee. Go to see it and take cash, not check, then negotiate them down on their price.

True Story:

My sister-in-law, Sharon, and I started our Home Day Cares at the same time. We both were desperately in need of furniture. She saw an Ad in the paper about a Day Care Center wanting to get rid of their old furniture. She called about it and we went to check it out.

In the basement of the facility, were literally hundreds of cots, child size desks, and cribs that were not in use. They were taking up space and needed to be removed. The Owner had purchased all new equipment and furniture, and wanted the old stuff out. There was nothing wrong with this stuff, nothing that a little soap and water couldn't cure.

The Owner sold us 4 cots a piece for about $8.00 each. Over the phone she said $10.00. If you were to purchase these cots from a store they would cost more than $30.00 each. So we loaded Sharon's car with the cots and went on our way. I called a few days later to see if the Owner still had the cribs that I saw. She had 3 left. I was able to buy all 3 for a little more than $50.00 along with 4 more cots for the same $8.00 each. I then got a call from a friend of my husband to come and get their baby stuff from his garage. I was able to buy from this guy, 2 high chairs, 2 swings, a play pen a bag of toys and a walker all for $25.00!

And just like furniture, everyone knows someone who has toys that their children no longer use. You can find toys anywhere. You can even go to resale shops and pick up trucks and little cars and baby dolls for little or nothing. And you can ask friends and relatives for the toys their children no longer use. Check them to make sure there are no loose or missing pieces. In general make sure the used toys are safe and suitable for the ages of the children that you care for.

Take the cardboard from an empty toilet paper roll and use it to check for dangerously small toys that could be a potential choking hazard. If the toy is small enough to fit inside the roll, it is too small for the children to play with and should be discarded.

Just be sure to wash them down with your bleach solution and allow to air dry. Then you can go to one of the super stores and purchase one of those all-purpose huge plastic bright colored drums to store your toys in. The children will not only like to dump the toys out but they will love to roll inside the drum as well, just make sure it doesn't have a lid on it. And don't forget the children's books. Find them; buy them; borrow them. You'll really want to read to the children as often as you can.

As your finances increase you can purchase new items for your children for both indoors and outdoors. When the whether is nice, you'll want to take them outside for fresh air. You can put the little ones in a stroller and the toddlers can play with balls and ride on tricycles and slides. It'll be up to you if you want to purchase a full swing set. But after you begin, you'll know in what direction you want to take your Day Care.

You may be fortunate enough to have at your local Human Development Center a Toy Library. If you do, you might be able to rent almost any piece of furniture, toys, books, puzzles, etc....through their Library. This is to help you get over the hump so-to-speak, if you temporarily don't have what you need or you want your children to try a new book or puzzle for a short period of time. This service, if it is available to you, may only cost a few pennies a year.

So now, don't become overwhelmed because you don't have everything right now. You WILL eventually have all that you need. Just start talking and the word will spread. Opportunities will open to you. Take it a step at a time. You'll do fine.

Chapter 3
Legal Frustrations

Legal Frustrations

While you are awaiting your License from DCFS, you can now begin your trip down the LEGAL HOME BUSINESS Lane. One of the very first things you'll want to do is call your County Clerks Office in your county, (remember, your state may have a different procedure). Tell them that you want Assumed Business Name forms for your small business. What this is, is a form that you fill out that will eventually be published in a major Newspaper for the purpose of locating someone else with your same business name. If no one responds, the name is yours.

So while you are waiting for these forms to come in, think of a Day Care name. For example, let's use "TOT VILLE, USA." So, John and Mary Smith are going to open a Day Care in their home called "Tot Ville, USA." Their Assumed Name forms finally come in the mail, (Example E and F). These forms in particular are for persons conducting a business as a "Sole Proprietorship." If you are planning to become a Corporation, then you'll have to check with your state and go through that process. Even this "sole proprietorship" process as well as the forms might be different in your state; however, "sole proprietorship is what you want. Now if you want to hire a Lawyer, form a Board of Directors and divide up Shares of your business; then go that route. We small home business persons have chosen, "sole proprietorship." And I think it's best, because you have to start somewhere small and learn the ropes before you become big.

Every county and state is of course different so you may not be asked about being a "Sole Proprietorship." You can always become a "Corporation" later. The objective is to get your business up and running and legal, for now.

Now, the Assumed Name form is pretty simple to fill out. John and Mary are asked to fill out what type of business they will have, the name of their business and the address of their business. They are asked the names of all persons owning and conducting such business.

Before they sign it, the two of them must go together to a Notary Public, usually at a Currency Exchange or a Village Hall; and they sign it in front of the Clerk. The Notary Public fills his/her part out and signs, dates and stamps the bottom portion. Then John and Mary will put this form in an envelope along with $5.00, check or money order, in some places it may be more or less, made out to The County Clerks Office of their county and mail it off. If the fee is different, your form will say so.

After it is received, you will get a notice in the mail that says something like the following document.

Notice

This is an acknowledgment that says that your *Assumed Name Certificate Form* has been received by the County clerks office of your county.

Assumed Name Publication Notice

Cert. #_____

NOTICE

Public Notice is hereby given that on _____, A.D. 19__.

a certificate was filed in the Office of the County Clerk of _____

County, Illinois, setting forth the names and residence addresses

of all persons owning, conducting and transacting the business

known as

_____,

located at

_____,

Dated this _____ day of _____, A.D. 19_____.

_____
County Clerk

Along with this notice, you may receive a list of newspapers to publish your Assumed Name for your county. If you don't receive this list, simply call a few of the more popular newspapers and ask for the classified for Assumed Names. Ask the price for publishing your Assumed Name and then tell them that you'll call them back.

Each newspaper has it's own price so don't spend more than you have to. After you've found the one that suits your pocket. Tell them that you'll fax your notice to them. Locate a fax and fax it. They will ask for payment in full so you can either give them your credit card number or mail them a check or money order before they will publish your notice.

The newspaper will publish your notice for 3 consecutive weeks. After that time they may send you a copy of the publication, (Example G and G 1). If they do, you then mail that publication back to the County Clerks Office. If they don't mail you this copy, they have already mailed it to the County Clerks Office for you. The County Clerk will issue you a file number and mail you back a Proof of Publication with your file number on it, (Example H). They will also mail you your CERTIFICATE OF OWNERSHIP OF BUSINESS, (Example I), and then you are done!

This is just an example of how it is done. Your state's procedures and certification may be a bit different. Nevertheless, you can now go to any bank with all of this information along with your identification and open a business account.

You are officially in business. Your professional title is:

LICENSED HOME DAY CARE PROVIDER!

Certificate

This form explains what kind of business you intend to have, the nature of your business, all people involved in owning the business and it's location. This is the form you will mail in so that you will receive your *Notice* of receipt of application of *Assumed Name Certificate*

State of_____)
County of_____)

File No._____
Filing Fee $5.00

CERTIFICATE

It is hereby certified that the undersigned is/are conducting or transacting Business under the Assumed name of:
_____
(List the Business Name)

The Business is being conducted at the following location:_____
_____
(List all Business Addresses located in the County)

The nature of the Business being conducted or transacted is_____
_____
(Declare the Type of Business)

The true and real full name of the person or persons owning, conducting, or transacting the business are as follows:

PRINT NAME

PRINT RESIDENCE ADDRESS

Dated this _____day of _____,19___

SIGNATURE_____

SIGNATURE_____

SIGNATURE_____

SIGNATURE_____
(All persons must sign)

State of_____)
County of_____) SS.

I,_____, a Notary Public in and for said County and State, do hereby certify that_____
is/are the same person(s) whose name(s) is/are subscribed to the foregoing instrument, and that _____
_____
appears before me this day in person and acknowledged that he/she/they has/have read and signed said instrument, and that each of the statements contained therein are true.

_____
(Notary Public Signature)

My commission expires on the _____day of_____, 19_____.

(Remember, your standard forms may be different from these.)

46

VITAL STATISTICS
ASSUMED BUSINESS NAME UNIT

COPY OF LEGAL NOTICE TO BE PUBLISHED

Notice is hereby given, pursuant to "An Act in relation to the use of an Assumed Business name in the conduct or transaction of Business in the State, as amended, that a certification was filed by the undersigned with the County clerk of *YOUR COUNTY.*

File No. _____ on the _____

(inserted by the County Clerk)

Under the Assumed Name of _____

_____

with the business located at _____

_____

The true name(s) and residence address of the owner(s) is:

_____

_____

_____

_____

Copy Of Legal Notice To Be Published

Even though you may not know your filing number, this form is filled out and mailed to the county clerks office along with the certificate. They will issue you a filing number when they mail this back to you. This is what the newspaper will use for publishing your *Assumed Name.* Mail this returned copy to the newspaper of your choice.

Certificate of Publication

This is an official certificate of the conclusive of your publication from the newspaper.

THE DAILY INTRUDER,
(an unreal name)

CERTIFICATE OF PUBLICATION

The Daily Intruder Company, (an unreal company), hereby certifies that it is the publisher of The Daily Intruder Newspaper, (an unreal name); it is an English language newspaper of general circulation, published daily in the City of Your City, County of Your County and the State of Your State; that The Daily Intruder has been so published continuously for more than one year prior to the date of first publication of the notice mentioned below and is further a newspaper as defined in Your State; that the undersigned person is the duly authorized agent of The Daily Intruder, (an unreal name), to execute this certificate on its behalf; and that a notice of which the annexed is an electronic copy was printed and published in said newspaper 3 times(s) and starting on: _____ and ending on; _____

Executed at Yours City, on _____

The Daily Intruder, (an unreal name)

by_____

_____
Notary Public   Date

Official Seal

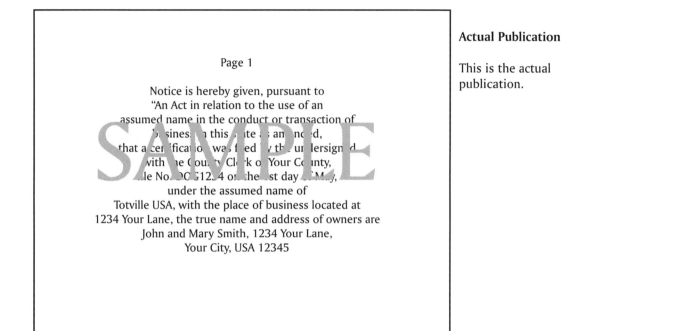

Page 1

Notice is hereby given, pursuant to
"An Act in relation to the use of an
assumed name in the conduct or transaction of
business in this state as amended,
that a certification was filed by the undersigned
with the County Clerk of Your County,
file No. DC 1234 on the 1st day of May,
under the assumed name of
Totville USA, with the place of business located at
1234 Your Lane, the true name and address of owners are
John and Mary Smith, 1234 Your Lane,
Your City, USA 12345

Actual Publication

This is the actual
publication.

Proof of Publication

This is the proof of your publication statement with your filing number on it that your county clerk's office will mail back to you.

RECEIPT FOR PROOF OF PUBLICATION

File No. _____

RECEIPT FOR PROOF OF PUBLICATION OF NOTICE OF OWNERSHIP OF BUSINESS

Receipt is hereby acknowledged of Proof of Publication of Notice of Ownership of Business,

pursuant to a Certificate filed in my office on

_____, A.D. 1____, _____

showing that such notice was duly published once each week for three successive weeks in the

_____, a secular newspaper of general circulation

regularly and continuously published in _____,

County of Your County, Your State, for more than one year last past, and that the first insertion

was on _____, A.D. 19_____, or

within 10 days after the filing of said certificate, and the last insertion on

_____, A.D. 19_____.

Dated this_____day of _____, A.D.

19_____.

_____

County Clerk of_____County, Your State.

STATE OF YOUR STATE
COUNTY OF YOUR COUNTY

FILING NO. 123456

APRIL 31, _____

Sample

Certificate of Ownership of Business

Name of Business: _____

Name of Owner: _____

Address of Business: _____

_____

Clerk

Certificate Of Ownership
This is the final certificate that says your business is registered by your state in the name that you
have chosen.

Chapter 4
Finding the Little Darlings

Finding the Little Darlings

The biggest concern most new Providers have is finding children. Let me tell you that it's a piece of cake. In a few weeks you could have more children than you can service knocking at your door!

Part 1: Guidelines

The maximum amount of children a Home Day Care Provider can care for varies from state to state. Generally it is 8 children under the age of 12 years. With no more than 5 children under the age of 5 and only 3 under the age of 2. **OR**, Up to 8 children under 12 with no more than 6 children under 5 only. **OR**, Up to 8 school aged children only.

It sounds difficult but the purpose is so that the children you care for have close, quality individualized care. Caring for more than that will not only drive you nuts but will produce lonely, angry children.

You may know of, or have heard of, many Providers who are *WAY* over the limit; and you, perhaps, want to follow that same road. Let me tell you, having more than the standard allowance is against the Law. Sure people do it all the time. And it's illegal, and in time, people get caught. When they are caught, they have a short amount of time to get rid of the overage and have to pay a stiff fine for collecting that money if the children were on public assistance.

The people who are over the limit most of the time are in it for the money. The sad thing is that their households have now depended upon this money and when they get caught, the income drastically drops and the household is then in a financial crisis.

There is no way to care for 22 children in a professional, close, and caring way. I'm not talking about a Group Home where you can have a bit more children with other rules and regulations, or a Day Care Center, but a basic Licensed Home Day Care. Now think about it. You will probably be propping the bottles in the infants mouths instead of cuddling them and feeding them the way their parents would. When in fact, that is what the parents are assuming you are doing. And the toddlers need even more quality care because they are the busy ones that get into everything.

You can't care for 12 infants and 10 toddlers at the same time. If you have help, you still are only allowed 8 children with the same guide lines, except you can have 4 additional children; and these additional children are school aged children only. If a parent assumes you are giving quality care to their child, and you are not, you are deceiving the parents and it's a matter of time before you are found out.

Of course you won't be doing EVERYTHING that a parent would, but they are under the assumption that you are coming close to what their children receive at home.

Parents need to be reassured that their little darlings are in good hands, so don't disappoint them. It will be hard, or in some cases, impossible to win their trust back.

You will get the cuddly Teddy Bear type of children that you could just eat up! You'll love to hug and squeeze them all the time and you'll find yourself running to their side every minute. You'll find them to be very obedient and you'll look forward to seeing them every day. They make it a joy to be a Provider. **BUT**…

Then You Will Also Get The Difficult Children!

You cannot spank them, no matter how much you may want to! You can put them in "Time Out". This is sitting them away from the other children for a period of 1 to 3 minutes. You should have a designated chair or spot that they go to and must sit in. It should not be a chair that they sit in to eat, or a play pen where they sleep. They will get mixed signals when you sit them in it, and they haven't done anything.

If you get a child who is irritatingly disobedient continuously, your job is to either deal with it and try to train them, or let them go. DCFS forbids corporal punishment of any kind. If you can't solve the problem with "Time Out" and would rather not train the child, then it would be better to let them go. Tell the parent you cannot handle their little darling and release them to find Day Care somewhere else.

Part 2: Assessing Your Area

You need to be aware of your area. Are you near a high school or a hospital? Are you in a quiet residential area or near a commercial area. Are the people in your area Upper Middle Class and White Collar Workers or Blue Collar Workers and Public Aid Recipients?

These things will help you determine just what kind of Day Care you'll have and what you will be able to charge a week for your services. You have to know what kind of parents you want to draw in and what will work for you. You also have to understand the needs of your own family so that your Day Care doesn't interfere with your home life.

So, let's suppose you live near a high school. You will then want to appeal to the teen mothers in the area. You will want to send a flier to the Principal, the Gym Coach, the Guidance Counselor and the Nurse in the school. You'll also tape up a flier at the local 24-hour convenience store and the Laundry Mat, and maybe, at the fast food restaurants in your area. You can also put an ad in your local newspaper appealing to Teen Mothers.

Remember, you want your flier to call out to Teen Mothers. They *NEED* you and your services! CALL OUT TO THEM. APPEAL TO THEM. And you will get them to respond to you.

There are many parents of pregnant teens that don't know that Public Aide will pay for their child care so that their teen parent can return to school. Many of them just accept that the teen's life is cut short because now they have this baby they must

support. It's your job to find out all of the services and agencies in your area that will help these teens pay for child care.

In your flier you will clearly state that YOU HELP TEENS GET BACK IN SCHOOL by providing them with information on child care payment programs set up by DCFS or whatever agency you have found for them. Talk with other teens. Call DCFS. These services are out there; you just have to dig them up.

And you can add boarders or copy pictures of balloons or children, or even animals. Just remember not to add too much. You want the words to be seen over everything else.

What if you live near a Hospital or 24-hour establishments? You know they're open all of the time; so, someone must need Child Care at night. You could have a Night Care service or even a Weekend service. Call these places and ask to put fliers up. Of course, these fliers should appeal to the adults. So make them as professional looking as possible. Not that the Teen fliers should be hand written, but the adults will only leave their children and spend their money on what looks like quality. Remember, you only get one chance to make a first impression.

And you don't have to spend a lot of money on the fliers, but make sure that whatever you spend, it's worth it. You can have someone with a computer do your flier and then you can take that copy to a self-serve copy store and make 50 or so copies. If you have a Printing Store make up your flier, it will be expensive. You will be charged for the typesetting and the printing as well. You can go to your Library and use their computer and make up the best flier you can with the software that they have and copy that. At least that will get you started. It might not be magnificent right now, but if it's at least decent and to the point, you'll get replies.

Let's say you have a background in Nursing. There is a market for ill children. The parents of these children find it hard to locate day care for them. You could rack up in this area. Ill or handicapped children need child care too! Look at your specialty or background and what you are willing to work with; and make up your flier from that.

Copy your fliers on *NEON* paper or at least colored paper. Never use plain white paper. Color says something about your business. Colored paper with black lettering will be nice enough. Don't go elaborate and have full color printing. It's not worth the time, effort and money. All people will do is throw them away after they have gotten the information.

When you go out to distribute your fliers, talk to the managers and supervisors to see if you can post a flier up in their cafeterias or in their front windows or somewhere visible to their customers and staff. Make sure to be courteous, even if they say "No". You may care for their child one day, because they remembered how nice you were.

Here are a few examples for you to follow. Make your fliers clean and to the point! If you place them in the right spots, you will have children "for days!" Watch and see!

TOT VILLE, USA

Licensed
Home Child Care

6wks. thru 12 yrs.
Monday thru Friday
DAY & NIGHT SHIFTS
(Ask For Details)

WE WORK WHILE YOU WORK!

We Also Help Teen Parents Get Back In School!

- ▸ Reasonable Rates, Daily, Weekly, Bi-Weekly, Monthly
- ▸ Accepting All Forms of Public Aide Programs
- ▸ CPR & Infant First Aide Certified
- ▸ Before & After School Care
- ▸ 3 Home Cooked "REAL" Meals &
  3 Snacks Served Daily
- ▸ Young Parent Program

Music, Dancing, Exercise, Story time, ABC's & 123's, Arts & Crafts, Movies, Fresh Air, Potty training, Hugs and Kisses

**WE PROMISE TO GIVE YOUR CHILD THE
BEST CARE POSSIBLE, JUST LIKE HOME!**

**HURRY! HURRY! DON'T DELAY!
YOU NEED TO CALL ON US TODAY!
709-123-4567**
SERVING MERRY VILLE AND SURROUNDING COMMUNITIES

You will notice that neither John and Mary's names nor their address were put on the fliers, only their phone number and general location. You don't want a would-be nut-case to have your name, address and phone number…The surrounding area is enough.

And one last thing…you can shrink your fliers to business card size putting 10 or 12 on a page of cover stock, which is heavier paper, and copy these or just pay to have basic business cards printed up. The basic ones don't cost much; but, **you need business cards!**

Chapter 5
The Contract

Bring diapers
Bring bottles
Bring clothes
Bring money
Leave on time

SIGN HERE
X

The Contract

Getting Them to Sign on the "X"

You **Must, Must, Must** have a contract for your Day Care. It is the backbone of your business. The contract is made up of the list of fees, what kind of things you want the parent to do, what you promise to do, what you will not tolerate, holidays and vacations and other rules and regulations that you want the parents to understand and follow.

This Day Care is in your home, and you don't want the parents coming into your home with their child telling you what you're going to do and what they won't do. This is your Business and you make the rules. If you have these rules written down and you have the parents sign it, you can always refer to it when you see trouble arising.

True Story:

A couple of years ago, I began keeping a newborn named Hank. His father, Henry Sr., and I went over the contract together. He agreed with everything at the time. He signed it and began bringing his son at 6:30 every morning. Soon his hours were changed at work, and instead of dropping him off at 6:30 a.m., he asked me if he could begin dropping him off at 5:00 a.m., because he now had to be at work by 5:30 a.m. He was a single parent trying to make ends meet so I said, "Sure", but no earlier than that. I knew he was doing the very best he could, so I didn't charge him extra for the extra time. I also gave him a break on my fees. Instead of charging him $110.00 per week, I charged him only $50.00 with the promise of an increase in 6 months. He was so very thankful.

Six months came and he was able to increase to $85.00 per week. He was paying each week on time. He was also bringing his baby on time every morning. I was there for his child every day. I got out of my bed each morning as promised and received his child every day without fail.

Time came around for his vacation. He felt that he should not pay me while he is away. I told him that in my contract which he agreed to and signed, states that he must pay me for his vacation time, however, he doesn't have to pay me for my vacation time. He was getting angry as he began telling me how unfair it was and that I should not charge for his vacation time, and also not charge for some of the national holidays that I take off. He also didn't want to be charged for the days he didn't bring his child. He literally wanted to change my contract for his benefit.

I told him, "**This business is my business**. If I change certain points of my contract for you, why then shouldn't I change to suit every other parent. I'm being less fair to myself and more favorable to you. Not only are you getting a break with the fees, you're not being charged for the 60 minutes overtime each morning. My Day Care begins at 6:00 a.m. not 5:00 a.m., yet I don't charge you for it. If I followed my rules to the letter, not only would you pay me $110.00 per week, but since I charge $1.00 per minute overtime, I would be charging you an extra $60.00 per day!"

"Do you go to a restaurant and change their rules and prices to suit you? Do you go to work and just decide to change their rules to suit you? Do you go to work and just decide to change their rules because you are uncomfortable? For the most part, if you don't like the rules at any given establishment, you simply move on, or just deal with it. If I change anything else, it will be my decision."

I also told him, "I would hate for you to take him out of my Day Care for this. I've cared for him for more than a year and he's attached to me. I take good care of him. If you want to take him out, it'll not be because he was treated badly. And anywhere else you may go will charge you more if they take him at 5:00 a.m. If you had a problem with my contract, you should have said something before you signed it. We could have discussed it back then." He was silent for a minute. "Do you understand my point? Do you still think I'm not being fair to you?" I asked him.

I wasn't loud and upset, I was merely standing on my contract and my promise to him. He said as he began to calm down, "Well, a…a…I see what you're saying and you are giving me a break. Well, okay. I see your point." And as he gathered up his child and began to leave I said, "See you in the morning!" He said with a grin, "Okay." And that was that.

You have to have something to stand on. Something to refer to. And in some instances, **something to hide behind** when all explanations fail! A contract keeps your parents for the most part, in order and it keeps you on track.

True Story:

I was doing 24-hour care for about a year before throwing in the towel. However, I encountered an interesting situation. I was caring for a child who's grandmother, the guardian, worked day and night shifts. She wanted me to keep the child for her night shift and would pick the child up in the morning, by 6:00 a.m. She got off at midnight and this would allow her to get some sleep before picking her granddaughter up.

During the day, she was cared for by another Provider who would drop her off at my house at 6:00 in the evening. The child was on Public Assistance which means that any overtime would have to come out of the grandmothers pocket.

I had only kept the child for a short period of time and days after registering the child with me the grandmother began her…"stuff"!

I was charging $1.00 a minute after 6:00 a.m. for the night shift and likewise, $1.00 per minute after 6:00 p.m. for the day shift. Ms. Grandma Molly was 100 minutes late picking up her granddaughter and had the nerve to get angry with me when she finally arrived dressed in her pajamas to pick her up.

I reminded her of my late fees and that she must pay them before the child could return. Well, she paid me by check…$20.00 for February, $20.00 for March, $20.00

for April and so on. She had given me 5 checks that were post dated and asked me if that was okay. This was in January.

I figured, well, okay. Let's help the woman out. She's stressed, she's tired. She's a single grandmother caring for this child and obviously carrying a host of other problems that I didn't want to know about. She asked me if I could call to wake her up so that she would not be late picking up her grandchild. I definitely told her "NO"! That was not my responsibility. It's her job to wake up and come and get this child. Well, she got mad at me. Yeah right!

Anyway, a couple of days went by and she was again late. Some 70 minutes late. The first check from the last episode hadn't even become available yet and she was late again. I quickly wrote her a letter canceling her child care. "A working relationship this does not make." I told her to just please take all of her checks back and find child care elsewhere. At the rate she was going, she'd owe me clear into the year 2000. I had to let her go quickly and didn't feel bad about it!

This is your business, so you decide what you will not tolerate. Don't hold onto a child because you're afraid you won't get another if you let that one go. I declare to you that you'll always have two more calling to replace the problem one.

Your contract is your business. You decide what you want to happen in your business and what you will not tolerate. The best way to put together a contract is simply to do it. After you do it and try to implement it, you'll see what you want to change. But you have to start somewhere. What Ms. Banana may have in her contract for her Day Care may not be what you want in yours. Here is a sample of a contract, use it to create your own.

You may choose to have a cover made and staple together a packet or simply put the whole thing in a colored folder. Or you may want to be really fancy and have it in full color with lively pictures. Do what works best for you and what is economical for your pocket. Be mindful that most of the parents will stash the contract away in a drawer after they have signed it. So the effort you put into the look of your contract is up to you.

You can make up a monthly newsletter to give them new information, or remind them of things already discussed. Or when you want to change any rules or regulations. Put it in a newsletter and hand it out to them. Keep a copy for yourself so that you can remember what information you gave them the month before. Please, don't be intimidated. This is your business, work it the best way you know how. Be yourself and trust yourself. You'll learn the best way to do things as you do them. And over the course of time, you'll change some things. You'll get better at things and, before you know it, you'll have it down pat!

TOTVILLE, U.S.A.

We promise to care for your child, perfectly!

Tot Ville, U.S.A.

LICENSED HOME DAY CARE

THIS CONTRACT AND CALENDAR THAT HAS BEEN PREPARED FOR

_____

Your New Fee is _____And Begins January 1, 1998

DAY SHIFT/NIGHT SHIFT

Monday thru Friday
IN ADDITION TO YOUR FEES BELOW,

THERE IS A $1.00 OVERTIME FEE FOR EVERY MINUTE IMMEDIATELY
AFTER YOUR ESTABLISHED CUTOFF TIME.

Exceptions are our discretion.

RATES

Registration Fee. . . . . $ 50.00
PER CHILD (NON-REFUNDABLE) THIS HOLDS YOUR SPACE FOR 15 DAYS.

Daily/Nightly Rate 35.00
(THIS IS CONSIDERED PART TIME. THERE IS NO HALF-DAY OR NIGHT RATE)

Sibling Daily/Nightly Rate Child 25.00
(EACH ADDITIONAL PART TIME CHILD)

Late Payment Fee 25.00
(FOR EACH OCCURRENCE)

Full time Infant 6wks to 2yrs. Weekly Rate (DAY OR NIGHT) 110.00

Full Time Toddler 2yrs to 3yrs Weekly Rate (DAY OR NIGHT) 95.00

Full Time Child 3yrs to 5yrs. Weekly rate (DAY OR NIGHT). 85.00

Full Time Child 6yrs and over Weekly rate (DAY OR NIGHT) 80.00

Sibling Rate Full Time Child Weekly Rate (1st SIBLING) 75.00

(2st FULL TIME SIBLING and EACH CHILD THERE AFTER $50.00)

Before and After School Care Flat Weekly Rate. 50.00
(PER CHILD. THIS RATE CHANGES TO FULL TIME RATE WHEN SCHOOL IS NOT IN SESSION.)

Co-Pay for Public Aide . . . . DCFS Rate
(THIS IS A MANDATORY FEE AND MUST BE PAID. NO EXCEPTIONS)

Part Time Care

Part time children come 3 days/nights or less per week. Fees are due IN ADVANCE each Friday for the coming week, ON TIME. If for personal reasons you are not bringing your child on any given day or week, YOUR REGULAR FULL PART-TIME PAYMENT FOR YOUR ONE CHILD IS STILL DUE AND FULL PART TIME PAYMENT FOR EACH ADDITIONAL CHILD IS ALSO DUE to keep your space in our Day Care. REMEMBER, YOU ARE PAYING FOR THE SPACE.

Full Time Care

Full time children come 4 or more days/nights per week. Fees are due IN ADVANCE each Friday for the coming week, ON TIME. REGARDLESS OF HOW MANY DAYS YOUR CHILD IS ABSENT, TO INSURE YOUR CHILD'S SPACE, YOUR FULL PAYMENT FOR YOUR CHILD/CHILDREN IS STILL DUE. YOU ARE PAYING FOR THE SPACE.

Co-Pay Fees

For TotVille to consider caring for your child, you must be full time. Consequently, you must pay your full time co-pay in full by the end of each month. If there is a reduction or increase in your fee, we will contact you immediately so that either we will be giving you back the difference or you can pay the difference. If your child is a day **and** night child, we will require an additional payment to cover your extra care as DCFS will not pay for the extra service, in which case, these fees must be paid at the end of the serviced week.

Should you decide to pay on your co-pay fees every two weeks to avoid a huge payment at the end of the month, that would be completely acceptable.

Missed Days, Late Payment And Overtime Fees

REGARDLESS OF HOW MANY DAYS YOUR CHILD IS ABSENT, INCLUDING YOUR DAYS OFF, YOU MUST PROVIDE EACH FULL DAY'S PAY FOR YOUR CHILD TO INSURE YOUR CHILD'S SPACE. LATE PAYMENT AND OVERTIME FEES ARE DUE AT THE TIME THE CHILD IS PICKED UP OR BY THE START OF THE NEXT SERVICE DAY. BRING YOUR CHILD EACH AND EVERY DAY, unless they are ill, it is a holiday or vacation time.

**YOUR CHILD MAY NOT RETURN
UNTIL YOUR BALANCE IS PAID IN FULL.**

I DO NOT HAVE A PROBLEM WITH ANYTHING ON THIS PAGE._____
(PARENTS INITIALS)

**ALL PAYMENTS MUST BE IN CASH AND ON TIME
—NO CHECKS ACCEPTED—**

Night Care:

Night care is any time between 6:00 p.m. and 6:00 a.m. the following day. Any time BEFORE or AFTER these hours is considered overtime and you will be charged an overtime fee, unless it has been established that you will be working these extended hours. In which case you will be charged your agreed rate.

We must be able to reach you at any given time **EVERY DAY**. Therefore, when you have days off, please do not bring your child as if you were going to work. We cannot reach you if you are out running errands, shopping, visiting and the like. Also, we want to encourage you to keep your child with you on your days off. Most of the time, your little one is with us more than he/she is with you and that is not good. If you must conduct business on your days off, we would appreciate it if you would keep your day short, give us your day's schedule and phone numbers where you can be reached; and then pick up your child as soon as possible. You are the parent and you only have one chance to enjoy them as children. Spend the time with them. A babysitter watches children. We are Licensed Day Care Providers. We care for your children while you are either working or in school.

Night care begins 6:00 p.m. Monday and extends through Saturday at 6:00 a.m. YOUR CHILD MUST-MUST-MUST BE PICKED UP on or before 6:00 a.m. ON SATURDAY on or before 6:00 a.m., NO EXCEPTIONS. If your child is not picked up on or before this time, you WILL be charged a $5.00 a minute fee and your child WILL NOT RETURN until this fee is paid-PERIOD!

THERE ARE NO SUNDAY HOURS...
THERE ARE NO SUNDAY HOURS...
NONE!

If your child is in our care through 2 shifts, (Day and Night), you will be charged accordingly. At no time will your child be allowed to remain in our care for more than a 24-hour period. We are the caregivers; you are the parent. Although we understand that you must do what you have to do to make a living, it is your job to figure it out. We cannot and will not replace the role of you as the parent so, please, be mindful that your child needs to be with you at home at some point every day.

When deciding to place your child with Tot Ville, to insure your child's space, YOU MUST PAY THE ONE TIME REGISTRATION FEE. REGULAR PAYMENT IS DUE EACH WEEK-EVEN IF YOUR CHILD HAS NOT YET STARTED. This is, of course, optional. If you would prefer, your name may go on the waiting list. However, space is limited and there may be a long list. The first to come is the first to be served.

I DO NOT HAVE A PROBLEM WITH ANYTHING ON THIS PAGE.____

(PARENTS INITIALS)

ALL PAYMENTS MUST BE IN CASH AND ON TIME
—NO CHECKS ACCEPTED—

We ask that you bring the following items every day.

- ❑ Bottles
- ❑ Blanket
- ❑ Formula—that is prepared for feeding
- ❑ Diapers
- ❑ Complete change of clothing
- ❑ Any personal ointment for sensitive skin

HOLIDAYS AND VACATIONS:
ALL HOLIDAYS ARE PAID HOLIDAYS AND ARE INCLUDED IN YOUR PAYMENT.
We are closed the following days this year:

New Years Eve   New Years Day and the Day After
Columbus Day   All Presidents Birthdays
Good Friday   Veterans Day
3 Weeks For Vacation During the Year   Memorial Day
4th of July Selected Day   Labor Day
Thanksgiving Day and the Friday After   Christmas Eve
Christmas Day

You are not expected to pay for our vacation time, however, **you are expected to pay us for your vacation time**. We will be closed for 3 weeks throughout the year for vacation. You will always be notified at least one month in advance. Please notify us of your vacations and days off.

Expectations For Public Aide Or Other Assisted Day Care:

We must have all necessary papers from your assisting agent in order to register your child. It is your responsibility to make sure all paperwork is filled out completely and mailed as soon as possible.

NEW DCFS Day Care Reform requires that you pay their standard co-pay fee to Tot Ville. This is based on your income and is deducted from our monthly paycheck. There are no exceptions. YOU MUST PAY YOUR CO-PAY IN FULL. It is due in full by the 30th of each month. Your child may not return if this co-pay is not paid in full at the time it is due, at which time, your child may return. However, you only have 7 days to pay this back co-pay before your child's care is terminated.

Until your assistance is activated, we require that you begin paying a co-payment fee. Upon activation, your payments will be adjusted. It is imperative that you pay your fee. DCFS takes your portion out of our paycheck, and requires us to collect this portion from you directly. This is your responsibility. We expect payment and all rules apply.

In the event, you are denied child care payment, we have collected something towards our services. If you are transferring from another facility, you do not have to pay the registration fee, however, you must begin paying your co-pay immediately.

We will require that your child be full time, 5 or more hours per day, at least 4 days a week for your assistance to be serviceable to us.

Missed Days, Late Payment And Overtime Fees:

Regardless of how many days your child is absent, including your days off, you must provide each full day's co-pay rate payment for your child to insure your child's space. Full late payment and overtime fees are due at the time the child is picked up or by the start of the next service day. Bring your child each and every day, unless they are ill, it is a holiday, or vacation time.

**YOUR CHILD MAY NOT RETURN UNTIL
YOUR BALANCE IS PAID IN FULL.**

Important Notice

We are no longer pleading with you to collect back payments.
we have decided to use the help of a
collection agency in order to collect for services rendered.

Please be advised that we will use any means necessary
to collect our payment.

So, please make all of your payments in full and on time.
Thank You

Summer Break:

Regardless of your school break, to insure your child's space with our Day Care, payment is still due each week throughout the summer. Your assisting agent will only pay for your child care if YOU ARE IN SCHOOL OR WORKING DURING THIS TIME.

It is your responsibility to find employment or attend summer school if you want your assisting agent to continue through the summer. YOUR SPACE IS NOT GUARANTEED should you decide to take your child out of our Day Care through the summer.

Payment rates and policies are subject to change at any time with at least 1 weeks notice.

We also reserve the right to terminate Day Care for your child/children at any time for reasons we feel are necessary and no refund will be given. If, for any reason, you terminate your child's care with us, a two-week notice must be given and there is no refund.

Enclosed are forms for you to fill out and return to **Tot Ville** along with the necessary fees before your child can be considered registered. Your registration fee only holds your space for 15 days unless you have begun weekly payments to hold your space until you are ready for child care. If you have not begun weekly payments after the 15 days, another $50.00 will be due to be considered registered if your space is available. NO SPACE IS GUARANTEED OVER THE PHONE. UNLESS YOU HOLD YOUR SPACE WITH CASH, IT IS FIRST COME FIRST SERVED!

All forms are required by the State of Illinois; so, please fill each one out completely. Sign, date and return all of them.

Health Requirement:

We require a health record for your child/children. Please be sure to keep up with your child's shots. We are not held responsible for illnesses your child may acquire as a result of negligent shots and regular check-ups.

If your child shows any of the following, you will have to make arrangements to keep your child at home: **PINK EYE, SEVERE COUGH, FEVER, INFECTED SKIN PATCHES, GRAY OR WHITE STOOL, DIARRHEA, UNUSUAL SKIN PATCHES, VOMITING OR SORE THROAT.**

If any of these symptoms develop while your child is in Day Care, they will be separated from the other children and you will be immediately called to make arrangements to have them picked up.

We are not available to cater to your sick child if you cannot take off from work or school. You must make other arrangements for your child until he/she recovers. **IT IS NOT FAIR TO EXPOSE THE OTHER CHILDREN TO YOUR CHILD'S ILLNESS, SO PLEASE BE RESPONSIBLE AND HAVE ALTERNATE CARE FOR YOUR CHILD UNTIL HE/SHE IS WELL.**

They will need a release from their doctor to return to Day Care if they have had a contagious illness. You are however, expected to maintain payment for your child's space. You will always be called **AND EXPECTED TO LEAVE WORK OR MAKE ARRANGEMENTS TO PICK YOUR CHILD UP** when your child shows signs of illness.

Meals:

Breakfast, Lunch, Dinner and three snacks are served daily for a full-time child. Aside from infant formula, we ask that your solid food eating child not bring any food or snacks or toys to Day Care.

Breakfast is before 9:00 a.m., lunch is before 12:00 p.m. and dinner is before 4:00 p.m. Snacks are served between these meal times. If your child comes after any of these times, they must wait for the next snack or meal time.

We are not responsible for lost or broken toys so please keep them at home. Pacifiers, bottles and diaper bags should be clearly identified.

Clothing And Potty Training:

A complete change of clothing is needed for each child daily. If your child is not potty trained, your are expected to furnish disposable diapers. We will not start potty training until your child is clearly ready, usually about 2 to 2 ½ years old. At that time we require that you purchase a toilet trainer, (one that sits on the floor), that will stay at Day Care for your child.

Diapers with re-stick tabs or Pull-ups should be worn until the child is completely trained. We ask that once you've begun to potty train your child, please continue through to the end. If not, it will only be confusing to the child and difficult for us. Please, no training pants or cloth diapers.

For services rendered to my child,_____, I, _____,
the undersigned, have read all and do agree to abide by all of the terms, conditions and procedures of
this contract between myself and TOT VILLE, U.S.A. day care. I understand that if I fail to pay any and
all parts of my agreed fee, TOT VILLE will take any means necessary to collect this debt.

_____

PARENT(S) SIGNATURE   DATE

_____

IN CASE OF EMERGENCY NAME   PHONE#   RELATIONSHIP

_____

PARENTS' NAME   ADDRESS   CITY   ZIP

_____

HOME #   WORK PHONE#   EXT.

_____

PAGER #   CEL-PHONE #   PUBLIC AIDE CASE #

_____

 SOCIAL SECURITY #   DRIVERS LICENSE #

MY NEW WEEKLY FEE IS $_____ MY CHILD IS SCHEDULED TO BE AT DAY CARE
FROM_____TO_____

IF THEY ARE AT DAY CARE OTHER THAN THESE TIMES, LATE FEES ARE ASSESSED.

For services rendered to my child,_____, I, _____, the undersigned, have read all and do agree to abide by all of the terms, conditions and procedures of this contract between myself and TOT VILLE day care.

At this time, I am agreeing to pay for the day care services of TOT VILLE the sum of $_____ per day/week until further notice. I understand that if I fail to pay any and all parts of my agreed fee, TOT VILLE will take any means necessary to collect this debt.

_____

PARENT(S) SIGNATURE   DATE

_____

DAY-CARE PROVIDER   DATE

MY CHILD IS SCHEDULED TO BE AT DAY CARE FROM_____TO_____.

IF THEY ARE AT DAY CARE OTHER THAN THESE TIMES, LATE FEES ARE ASSESSED.

PARENT'S COPY

General Daily Schedule

6:00 a.m.	Receive Children
6:30	Free Play/sleep
7:00	Breakfast/bathroom Break
9:00	Numbers/math/colors/shapes
	Alphabets/writing/phonics
10:00	Am Snack/bathroom Break
	Arts & Crafts
11:00	Quiet/story Time
11:30	Lunch/bathroom Break
12:00 p.m.	Nap
1:30	Pm Snack/bathroom Break
2:00	Music/dance/outside
3:30	Dinner/bathroom Break
4:00	Movie/free Play
5:30	Evening Snack/bathroom Break
6:00	CHILDREN GO HOME

Parents please note:

This is a general schedule. We flow with the children. Some days we will accomplish everything, and some days not at all. This is a **home** day care not a school, nor a center. We spend our time nurturing the children, anything else is secondary.

You may feel that this contract is a bit strict but after you've handled a few tough parents and their many different situations, you'll appreciate a rigid contract. You can, of course, alter it privately with each parent and their needs. Like the story I've just mentioned with Henry and Hank, he was only paying me $85.00 per week instead the regular fee of $110.00.

True Story:

I had another mother some years ago who needed child care desperately but could only afford $70.00 per week. She and her husband had just built a home, they had just had a baby and all was going well. The husband went out for cigarettes and never came back. She now had to find a job to pay the mortgage, pay a babysitter and make a decent living. I could not charge her my full rate. I told her that if I cut her rate she had to pay me in full every week without fail. No excuses, no I. O. U's. She was doing the very best she could. She kept her word.

Some parents, you just know are doing the very best they can. Your heart will go out to them and you may want to cut their rate. But, beware of the parent that would seek to get over on you.

True Story:

I gave a woman a cut rate because of her sob, sad sack story. She said she couldn't afford my then fee of $85.00 per week but she could afford $40.00. I said okay, but temporarily. And she began paying me on time. Her hair was done up every week. Her nails were done every week. She was dressed to the "Nines" every day. She had GOLD jewelry everywhere, all the time, and drove a fancy car that was clean every day! Now, I said to myself, what is wrong with this picture? Someone is not telling the truth!

I told her that I wanted to increase her fee by $5.00 every other week and she began to have problems. She was spreading her money rather thin and began having a hard time paying me the $40.00 each week. Her child was a newborn. He was a serious screamer and I was keeping him 8 to 10 hours every day. $40.00 a week just wasn't enough pay for me to put up with such a baby as that. She began to explain how she couldn't come up with all of the money. She had things in the layaway and she didn't have my Day Care money. But, I could get it from her father.

She was my next door neighbor. She was still living with her parents and never really had many responsibilities. Her parents were always her safety net. I told her to go and ask her father. It wasn't my responsibility to get it; it was hers. Well, one thing lead to another and she stopped bring her child…by my request.

> Some people you can give a break.
> Some people you can alter your contract for.

But,

> Some people need strict, firm rules.
> Some people need to know there are only two sides to your rules, **"YOUR SIDE OR THE OUTSIDE"**!

It's a shame, but some parents you come across will not have their priorities in order and will lie to you. In other words, their child care isn't that important. They don't quite understand that they need you so that they can go to work. They need you to care for their child so that they can attend school. If they didn't need you, they would have their child somewhere else. It is so important for you to present yourself in a professional non-wavering manner so that they won't attempt to bend your rules. Whether they be friend or family, **your business is your business**. Make that contract so you have something to stand on.

You will also find that some parents feel that you make enough money from your other parents, therefore, they can be given a break, you really don't need it. They don't see your Day Care as a business. They don't see you as a priority. They can pay you later, after all, you're just a "Baby Sitter"! When in fact, this is YOUR job, every day. People can become complicated, especially when it comes to their money and their children. This is your business and you are in this business to make money. You are not doing this for free!

True Story:

When our oldest son was a baby, my husband and I were both working outside of the home and depended on the neighborhood baby sitter to care for our child. Although she was not licensed, she had a basic contract and for the most part stuck with everything on it. Her fee was not much, just $40.00 per week and she was reliable.

The one thing she did stick with was her late fees. You must pick up your child on time or you must pay her fee of $5.00 for every 15 minutes you are late. You could not bring your child back until that late fee was paid.

Well, we were late picking up our son only once! But that one time was enough for us. We owed her perhaps $30.00 in late fees and didn't have it when we came to pick up our child. She said, "No problem, see you in the morning." So we thought, "no problem, we'll bring him in the morning as usual". We rang the bell that following morning and as always she answered the door. "Good morning, Mike-Mike", she said to our son. "And Good morning to you. You are paying your late fee this morning aren't you.?" "Well, no," we replied, "You said no problem last night." "Well," she said very sternly, "it wasn't a problem last night, but it is today. Here," she handed my child back, "Go and get your late fee and come back. He can't come back until your late fee is paid, PERIOD!"

That was her rule and that was that, her side or the outside! We found some money quick, fast and in a hurry! We had to go to work.

Get that contract together and stick to it. If you change anything, let it be on YOUR TERMS ONLY!!!!

Remember,

It's your side or the outside!

Chapter 6
The Main Reason Why We Do This Every Day

The Main Reason Why We Do This Every Day

It's simple, we do this for *THE MONEY*! And the love of children, hoping to get paid a decent dollar for all of our efforts. We have to enjoy caring for other people's children, but because we know that we'll be rewarded for this, we'll gladly do it Monday through Friday, 6:00 a.m. to 6:00 p.m.

What is the appropriate amount to charge parents? How do I get Public Aid children? Which is the better deal? Do I give out receipts? Do I claim my income on my taxes? How much do I pay my assistant? I could go on and on with the zillions of money questions. I'll answer the ones listed and maybe a few more.

Part 1: What Do I Charge?

What you have to do is a little simple research. Check around in your area at other Day Care Centers as well as Home Day Care. You may be able to obtain a listing from your local DCFS, and find out what they are charging and beat their price. Let's say the Learning Bridge Center around the corner from you is charging $145.00 per week for infants and $115.00 per week for 2 years and up. The Homes in your area are charging $110.00 for infants and $95.00 for 2 years and up. So perhaps you could charge $85.00 per week for infants and $75.00 per week for 2 years and up. It's really up to you. You want to be competitive but fair to yourself. With the centers like these around you, don't charge $40.00 or $60.00 per week. You won't make as much money as you could be making.

You may also check to see if you have some sort of Home Day Care Resource/Referral Service available to you. They may know what the average rate is in your area. And they can also help you in locating children as well. If you locate this service in your area, register your Day Care with them. The people who call this service get the list of providers in their area and the fees they charge. When they call you, they already know what you will be charging them and are probably willing to pay it.

Have your parents pay you at the beginning of the week for the first week so that you won't have a frustrating situation on your hands. You don't want to have cared for a child all week and then the parent says that you have to wait 2 weeks from next Thursday to be paid for this past week because the car broke down, the grandmother died and the cat ran away! "I'm really sorry, but really, you'll get your money, I promise!" They say it, but 9 times out of 10 you'll never see it if you don't take further action. We'll discuss going after that back money in a few minutes.

Things happen and situations come up. My advice to you is get paid ahead of time and there will be no problems. And if you've already stated no refund, and they never return after the first day, you've at least been paid for the one week. Also, get the Registration Fee, even if it's $25.00 dollars, you'll want to hold their space for the time stated in your contract. You may want to purchase extra wipes or a new spray bottle or nothing at all. That Registration money is for your efforts. So, collect the Registration money at the beginning of the first week. And there after, collect your fee every week for the coming week.

Do not allow the parents to pay you with a check. If it bounces you have your bounced fee to pay and on top of that you have to wait for them to pay you again. Always collect cash. And when they pay you, right it down in some sort of receipt book. You can purchase one from any office supply or super store for about $5 or $6 dollars. I have found that the "Money/Rent Receipt 2-Part books work best because you tear off the top copy for the parent and the copy you need is kept in the book. The receipt looks something like this:

Receipt Date _____ 19 _____ **No. 000001**			
From_____$			
_____DOLLARS			
FOR RENT			
FOR_____			
FROM_____TO_____			
ACCT_____ _ CASH			
PAID_____ _CHECK			
DUE _____ _MONEY			
_ORDER BY_____			

You'll also need this for taxes so get that book.

You'll want to keep a chart of who has paid you and who has not for each month. You WILL get confused if you don't keep track of the "Loot"! The table could look something like this:

July	Byrd	Wicks	Jones	Davis	Cox	Gills	Tate
1	$85.00	85.00	85.00	75.00	75.00	75.00	50.00 75.00
8	85.00	85.00	85.00	75.00	75.00	75.00	75.00
15	85.00	85.00	85.00	75.00	75.00	75.00	75.00
22	0	85.00	85.00	75.00	75.00	75.00	75.00
29	25.00 170.00	85.00	85.00	75.00	75.00	75.00	75.00
Total	450.00	425.00	425.00	375.00	375.00	375.00	425.00

MY TOTAL FOR THE MONTH IS: $2850.00

Here you can see that the late fee has been applied and the registration fee has been collected. This particular month's total was very good. You will have the receipts to back this total up. It doesn't have to be just like this one, just make sure that you can keep a good organized record of your income.

There are of course other ways to keep a record of your income as well as the daily attendance of your children. Here are a couple of more ideas. You may even begin to make up your own method of record keeping. There is no real right way of keeping records. What ever works best for you is the best way of keeping your records.

DAILY ATTENDANCE FOR EACH CHILD

Childs Name_____   Month_____

Mon	Tues	Wed	Thurs	Fri	Sat	Sun	Payment

Notes_____

_____

_____

_____

_____

_____

_____

_____

_____

_____

_____

_____

Or you may want to keep a monthly record like this:

Monthly Attendance

For the month of:_____ Year_____ Total amount of eligible days____ (Mon thru Fri)

Childs Name _____ Total Fees expected for the month_ _____ Balance due from last month_____

Total Fees collected for the month_____ Balance paid from last month_____

| 1 | 2 | 3 | 4 | 5 | 6 | 7 | 8 | 9 | 10 | 11 | 12 | 13 | 14 | 15 | 16 | 17 | 18 | 19 | 20 | 21 | 22 | 23 | 24 | 25 | 26 | 27 | 28 | 29 | 30 | 31 |

Childs Name _____ Total Fees expected for the month_____ Balance dure from last month_____

Total Fees collected for the month_____ Balance paid from last month_____

| 1 | 2 | 3 | 4 | 5 | 6 | 7 | 8 | 9 | 10 | 11 | 12 | 13 | 14 | 15 | 16 | 17 | 18 | 19 | 20 | 21 | 22 | 23 | 24 | 25 | 26 | 27 | 28 | 29 | 30 | 31 |

Childs Name _____ Total Fees expected for the month_____ Balance dure from last month_____

Total Fees collected for the month_____ Balance paid from last month_____

| 1 | 2 | 3 | 4 | 5 | 6 | 7 | 8 | 9 | 10 | 11 | 12 | 13 | 14 | 15 | 16 | 17 | 18 | 19 | 20 | 21 | 22 | 23 | 24 | 25 | 26 | 27 | 28 | 29 | 30 | 31 |

Childs Name _____ Total Fees expected for the month_____ Balance dure from last month_____

Total Fees collected for the month_____ Balance paid from last month_____

| 1 | 2 | 3 | 4 | 5 | 6 | 7 | 8 | 9 | 10 | 11 | 12 | 13 | 14 | 15 | 16 | 17 | 18 | 19 | 20 | 21 | 22 | 23 | 24 | 25 | 26 | 27 | 28 | 29 | 30 | 31 |

Childs Name _____ Total Fees expected for the month_____ Balance dure from last month_____

Total Fees collected for the month_____ Balance paid from last month_____

| 1 | 2 | 3 | 4 | 5 | 6 | 7 | 8 | 9 | 10 | 11 | 12 | 13 | 14 | 15 | 16 | 17 | 18 | 19 | 20 | 21 | 22 | 23 | 24 | 25 | 26 | 27 | 28 | 29 | 30 | 31 |

Childs Name _____ Total Fees expected for the month_____ Balance dure from last month_____

Total Fees collected for the month_____ Balance paid from last month_____

| 1 | 2 | 3 | 4 | 5 | 6 | 7 | 8 | 9 | 10 | 11 | 12 | 13 | 14 | 15 | 16 | 17 | 18 | 19 | 20 | 21 | 22 | 23 | 24 | 25 | 26 | 27 | 28 | 29 | 30 | 31 |

Childs Name _____ Total Fees expected for the month_____ Balance dure from last month_____

Total Fees collected for the month_____ Balance paid from last month_____

| 1 | 2 | 3 | 4 | 5 | 6 | 7 | 8 | 9 | 10 | 11 | 12 | 13 | 14 | 15 | 16 | 17 | 18 | 19 | 20 | 21 | 22 | 23 | 24 | 25 | 26 | 27 | 28 | 29 | 30 | 31 |

Childs Name _____ Total Fees expected for the month_____ Balance dure from last month_____

Total Fees collected for the month_____ Balance paid from last month_____

| 1 | 2 | 3 | 4 | 5 | 6 | 7 | 8 | 9 | 10 | 11 | 12 | 13 | 14 | 15 | 16 | 17 | 18 | 19 | 20 | 21 | 22 | 23 | 24 | 25 | 26 | 27 | 28 | 29 | 30 | 31 |

Perhaps this may work for you:

Payments Made for the Month of_____

Childs Name	Govnm't Check	Co-Pay Total	Total Cash	Wk #1	Wk #2	Wk #3	Wk #4	Wk #5

Notes_____

_____

_____

_____

_____

_____

_____

_____

_____

_____

_____

Do what works best for you. Remember there is no right or wrong way to record. Just make sure that you do record both your attendance and income weekly.

Also, out of the 8 children you will have, you'll want to have at least 4 cash paying parents. The other 4 can be from Public Aid parents. You'll want cash in your pocket each week, and the rest of your income might come from an Assisting Agent at the end of each month.

Part 2: Public Aid Children

When you do your advertising, you'll get phone calls inquiring about your Day Care. You'll ask them if they are on Public Aid. If they say no, then you continue with what you want to know from them about their child and when they want to start. If they say yes, they are on Public Aid, then you begin to ask them if they have a CASE NUMBER. If they do not, you cannot classify them as being on Public Aid.

If they do have this number, they need to go to their Case Worker and get the Public Aid Day Care Payment forms for both you and them to fill out. If they have been to any previous Day Care facilities, then you are only transferring their information to your Day Care. If not, you simply fill out you part of the information and have them fill out their part WITH YOU and then remember to sign your name, and have them sign as well. I prefer to mail the paperwork myself, especially if they are young and seem to be "flighty in the head, or irresponsible."

You don't want anything delaying the processing of your money, therefore, you can mail out the forms to be sure that it is done. At this time, you begin charging your cut rate fee. **Only charge this fee if they are <u>not</u> transferring from another facility.** They have already been approved for payment if they were at another facility. So you WILL be paid. But there is one downfall to having Public Aid children and some Providers would rather not deal with it. It's this. When you have filled out all of the forms and have mailed them all in, for your very first paycheck, you may have to wait anywhere from 45 to 60 days. However, you are approved and it is coming. Hopefully, you have enough paying parents that will carry you through until you begin getting your checks. After that, they come usually on time.

Be careful to quickly mail out the forms when you get them, because when the parent transfers to your Day Care, the other facility still gets that child's attendance form and they may fill it out, forge the parents signature and mail it in even though you are now keeping the child. The government doesn't always catch the change right away and will send your money to them and you'll never get that check. If this does happen, you must call the Public Aid paying agent and tell them the situation so that they can pull the case file and go over it. They will then send you out another attendance form which will take another 45 to 60 days.

The attendance form looks something like this:

Date of issue: 3/31/1998

Page 1 of 1
For the month of March, 1998

Department of Human Services

CHILD CARE CERTIFICATE

This will certify that the provider listed below has been approved for the payment of child care benefits for the Month listed above.

Payment for this child care will be made on behalf of the client listed below.

Betty Davis
12345 East West Street
Any Village, USA 12345-6789

Jackson, Veronica
98765 West East Street
Any Town, USA 98765-4321

Name of child	Date of Birth	Rate	Eligible Days	Total
Jack Jackson	03/09/1993	$13.30 X	22	= $266.00
		$ 8.62 X		=

Total Charge $266.00
Monthly Parent Co-Pay   - 66.00
Total To Be Paid $200.00

PROVIDER MUST COMPLETE THIS SHADED AREA AND SIGN THE FORM.
(Count only those days the child was present.)
Number of Days Attended for the month.

Full Time [ ]   Enter the total number of days the child was in your care for 5 hours or more during the month.

Part Time [ ]   Enter the total number of days the child was in your care for less than 5 hours during the month.

THE PROVIDER IS RESPONSIBLE FOR COLLECTING THE PARENT CO-PAYMENT.

If the children attended for less than 80% of eligible days, payment will be based on the number of days attended.

If you are no longer providing care for the family, what was the last date you cared for the child?

[ ]

You cannot charge a parent receiving subsidized child care a higher rate than you charge your private paying clients.

I certify that the information submitted above is complete and accurate. I understand giving false information or failure to provide correct information can result in referral for prosecution for fraud.

Provider's Signature [ ]

Daytime Phone # [ ]

CLIENT MUST SIGN THIS FORM
I certify that this information is an accurate statement of child care provided due to my employment. I understand giving false information or failure to provide correct information can result in referral for prosecution for fraud.

Clients Signature [ ]

Daytime Phone # [ ]

Mail the completed form to:

Child Care and You
Department of Children and Parent aide
12345 SW North Street
Your Town, USA 12345-6789

(Remember, your forms and instructions may be different.)

Child Care Certificate

This is an approved form from your local Department Of Children and Family Services that you have previously set up with the mother that you must fill out at the end of the month and return to them in order for you to receive a paycheck for your Public Aid children.

The good side to Public Aid payments are that once all of the kinks are removed and the child is now registered with you, you will receive forms on time and when you mail them out at the end of the month, you will get that month's check at the end of the next month, give or take 5 days or so.

Let me say too that Public Aid Day Care payment policies are changing over and over. So currently, there is what's called a co-pay fee that the parents now have to pay. DCFS will pay their portion and the parents must pay the balance.

For instance, where they, (DCFS), used to pay $400.00 per month for little Rebecca Martin, they now may only pay $325.00 and the parent must come up with the $75.00 difference. And you have to make them pay this amount. It is taken out of your check so you must get it from your parent.

The amount that they owe you will show up on your attendance form that you receive each month. Show your parents their fees and let them know that you will be expecting this payment in a few days or however you've worked it out with your parents. It might not sound like $75.00 a month is much at all, but for a DCFS client to now be held responsible for a portion of their child care, it's a big deal to them.

This co-pay is figured based on the parents income. If you don't collect it from them, you won't get it. It's your responsibility to teach your parents how to treat you. Don't be sloppy with collecting your fees. If you are, you'll be paid sloppily by all of your parents and you'll never be paid in full.

Public Aid pays okay. They have their own rates, (which may change), based on your county or state so in some instances they may pay more or less than your current rates. If they pay more, then you must increase your rates. But, if less, then you can leave your rates where they are. Public Aids payment policy states that you can't charge your paying clients less than Public Aid will pay.

So for example, if Public Aid gives you $404.00 per month for an infant, you can't charge a paying mother $275.00 per month for the same age infant. Public Aid feels then they are paying you too much. So, if they pay you $404.00 per month, which is $101.00 per week, you have to charge at least that to satisfy Public Aid.

No one is saying that you can't work with a mother who is struggling to make ends meet. If she has to start off paying you say, $85.00 per week and then over a period of time work her way up to $105.00 per week, or whatever your full rate of pay is, then that is okay, as long as it is written somewhere in an agreement that you keep in the child's file.

There are so many branches of the Public Aid child care payment program as well as many programs available to very young mothers who aren't on Public Aid. At some point you may come across a mother who can't pay and has no idea of the programs available to her. For instance, there is a program for teen mothers called OPPORTUNITIES. This branch caters to young mothers up to age 25. There is also, TITLE TWENTY which pays for children 2½ and older. HEALTHY MOMS / HEALTHY KIDS pays for infants through 2½ years old. Both of these programs have very strict stipulations but they pay equally as well. PROJECT CHANCE is yet another program to help young mothers. And the list goes on and on. Check in your county or state for what programs are available. They may have different names, so as you hear of one, and there are many, just jot it down and keep it for a later use.

True Story:

A few years ago, while I was rocking one of my Day Care babies to sleep, I noticed this young girl sitting on a lawn chair in the driveway of the house a few doors down from me. She had a very small baby with her, in it's car seat. I stood at my window and watched her for a few days. After about the 4th day, I couldn't stand it. It was the end of the summer and most of the young girls her age had gone back to school. While my assistant cared for the children, I walked down to where she was and I asked her who she was. I'd been in the neighborhood 8 years and had never seen her before. I also asked her who's baby did she have because surely it couldn't be hers.

She replied in this soft baby like voice, "She's my baby." Well, I almost fell over. I asked her how old was she. "12 goin' on 13," she said so innocently. I was stuck. What could I say next? Here is a baby with a baby and she had no idea of what to do with this little life. I asked her about returning back to school and what grade she was in. She said with broken English, "Well, I don't have no baby sitter for my baby so I can't start the 8th grade yet."

"Baby, baby," I said, "Where is your mother?" She said, "I live here with my grand-daddy and his wife and her son, Bernardo. He's my baby's daddy and he's 'almost to be' 14! My Mama is workin' and lookin' for us a place. So for now, I live here." All I could do was shake my head.

I had to take her by the hand and call one of these Public Aid branches for her because this child couldn't do it. She was able to get someone to take her to the office to pick up the forms. We filled them out and I mailed them. She was so happy to begin school. However, the joy didn't last long. She couldn't get it together with diapers and lunch, baths and books and formula and homework. She virtually had no one, not the baby's father, not her grandfather, not even her step-grandmother helping her.

The baby was now about 2½ months old and she was squeezing her into the 2 or 3 newborn clothes that she had. She had cut the feet out of the sleepers so that they would fit. My heart went out to her but there was only so much I was going to do for her. Somewhere, her guardians would have to step in and take over. She obviously couldn't do this child raising thing! She didn't have a clue as to what she was doing with this baby.

The baby was always in bad need of a bath and my husband told me not to help her with anything outside of Day Care because he knew that if I started bathing, etc…, this young mother would always expect me to do it. I could only tell her the things that needed to be done.

She had a grandfather and step-grandmother and other relatives in that house who could help her. They were able-bodied people. There were also other women and other friends of these grown people coming and going in the home. I just couldn't take on that responsibility to help her any more than I was. And the sad point was after all of this, this young girl dropped out of school to be with her drop out boy-friend that she was living with. It was too much for her to be a Mom at 13. One day she stopped coming. I called and called, even visited the home. A man answered the door and said that she had quit school and she and the boy moved to Indiana to live with her mother.

Sometimes you can help get a mother on a program that will help her, but the home life is so very tragic that you simply can do nothing about it. Sometimes, you can help get a mother on a program and you look up, and because of you, she has made a success of her life. Sometimes, it's that little assistance that means all the difference in the world.

True Story:

I was approached in church some time ago by a young girl who had a baby and needed child care so that she could return to school. I had the space and took the child the very next day. She had some money from an inheritance so she was able to pay weekly. I, however, suggested that she seek out one of the available programs so that she could save that money for her future.

She was able to get on HEALTHY MOMS / HEALTHY KIDS. While on this program, she needed a place to stay because she was in fact an orphan and was not able to live with any of her relatives. So we took her in and helped her to raise her baby. She was 17 years old at the time and her baby was 6 months. Time went on and because we helped this child recover her life not only with the Day Care program available to her but with our love and support and including her in our family unit, she has gone to college, and has owned and operated a thriving Cellular business. Recently she made the decision to close her business and become my assistant.

Your help makes all the difference in the world, sometimes.

Part 3: Careful Selection

You may decide you only want to keep a certain type of child, you can't. Because you are licensed by the Government you cannot discriminate against any type of child, including ill or handicapped children, because you have a state approved license. You may, however, decide to increase your fees because that ill or handi-capped child will require far more time and attention from you than the average child. If the parent is willing to pay your fee then that is fine. However, let's not make it some astronomical fee that only "The Angels in Heaven" can pay!

You can decide what age group you'd rather care for keeping within the guidelines of your local DCFS. In other words, you cannot have 8 infants. If you'd rather care for only infants, you can only have the amount that DCFS allows. And likewise with toddlers.

True Story:

Some years ago, I had a Provider friend who no longer wanted to care for infants. Any parent who would call inquiring about Child Care for their infant wouldn't get a flat out "No," instead, she would charge a much higher rate for caring for their child in hopes they would look elsewhere. In the event they didn't and wanted her services badly enough, she would get paid a good price for the infant care.

All of her other children had grown up and were walking and talking. She was able to go on many field trips and do all kinds of new things with them because they all were older. With infants she would have to carry bottles and diapers and deal with the crying and other things that she didn't want to deal with anymore.

If a parent has an ill or handicapped child, be honest with yourself and the parent. These children sometimes need specialized care that you may not be able or have the ability to provide. Don't tell the parent that you will care for their child just

because you will be paid more. You will do more harm to the child if you cannot provide the services the child needs.

Just remember to stay within the guidelines of DCFS. You never want to be reported because of discrimination. That wouldn't be good.

Part 4: Paying My Assistant

If you really need an assistant, get an assistant. He/she should be responsible, over 18 years old and without a police record. They will have to fill out background check forms and get their finger prints just like you have done. They will become licensed as well, but only in your home.

You decide what time of the day you need them, but you can't expect them to put in the same twelve hours that you put in and not get paid what you get paid. If you need the money, don't split it unless you can afford it. They will expect something decent just as you would.

You may be fortunate to have a volunteer person to come in 3 or 4 hours a day to play with the kids and occupy them while you get lunches done and clean up a little bit. However, they too must be approved of by DCFS to be around your Day Care Children.

True Story:

I currently know of a Provider who is fortunate enough to hire an elderly lady to come in and cook, clean up around the house, (nothing major), wash clothes as she feels up to it and rocks the babies while she does the other stuff. The woman gets paid about $200.00 per week for 6 hours a day, Monday through Friday.

I know of another Provider who had a young woman come in and volunteer 5 hours a day, Monday through Friday. This young girl felt that each would be doing the

other a favor. The young girl was pregnant and had never been around little children before. The Provider needed help, so the two helped each other out. The young girl learned patience and all the details of handling little children and the Provider got much needed help for free!

There are of course so many other instances where an assistant is so needed and you have to decide for yourself the level of help you really need. And you may need to compromise on what you are willing to pay and what they are willing to accept.

I know of still another Provider who hired an assistant with a child of her own. The child, in fact, took up space, so their agreement was that she could bring her child and the money the Provider would be getting if that were a paying child is deducted each week from the assistant's income. The child must eat so that too is deducted and what is left is the assistant's pay.

So for instance, if the agreement was $250.00 a week. And the regular weekly fee is $110.00, that leaves $140.00. Subtract 3 meals and 3 snacks, wipes and tissue, the assistant gets about $120.00 per week. She is happy with that because she gets to spend time with her son. So it works out in this situation.

Every Day Care is different. If you don't do much but watch them play, change diapers, cuddle and tickle, sing songs, meals, naps and movies, then it won't be a heck of a lot you will pay out because there isn't a heck of a lot to do. However, if you go on field trips every week, you have a rigorous academic schedule for the children, they are outdoors every day-rain or shine; gymnastics, gourmet meals, piano lessons, heavy duty arts and crafts and the like, then expect to fork over a nice sum each week.

Whatever you pay out, just make sure that you pay yourself more! As the owner, operator of your Home Day Care, you should be paid more than your employee. And it's up to you to decide when to pay them. You get paid each week, perhaps pay them each week. You get paid monthly, they then get paid monthly. What you can do is if you have sufficient enough children and all of your bills and expenses are covered, you can give the income from one of your children to your helper. That way, the child is actually paying for the helper, not you. Just be fair and get an understanding right from the start!

And talk with an Accountant concerning your employee. Make sure all of your bases are covered so you won't have problems come tax time.

Part 5: Going After That Back Pay

It's unfortunate but sometimes you just have to "get the Bloodhounds out to go after your money". You may not want to do it, but when all else fails, especially if you've rendered a month or more of service and have not been paid anything for it, you must do it.

Sometimes it's just plain ignorance. You might not have really known that the parent had no intention of ever paying you and you just couldn't say no. I've heard over and over again, "But they really had this sob story and they needed someone to watch their kid." Dog-gone-it, why you? Don't be taken by these stories. They are invented to make you feel responsible and guilty at the same time. When you understand that your time is money, you won't let someone else disrespect your time in place of money.

But sometimes non- payment can't be avoided. Sometimes people have situations that cannot be helped and they simply can't pay as agreed. In that case, you must make a repayment plan to get them caught up.

Sit down with them and honestly discuss how to go about correcting this. If it is not corrected soon, they will become further and further behind and they can't catch up. Then you are stuck between obligation to them or plain 'ol loss of those payments. It becomes easy to say, "just forget it. But next time….", and the next time comes over and over again and you don't do anything about it. STOP IT!!!!!!!!!!

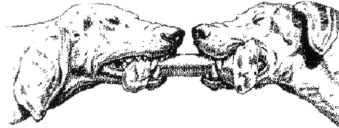

Teach them now how to treat you. Your payments are mandatory, even the unforeseen back payments, these must be paid, PERIOD. NO QUESTION ABOUT IT!

I've had parents who said that they were struggling to pay me during the Holiday season. Obviously they were alluding to not paying me so that they could finish their Christmas shopping. If I let them, they'll take my payment and go out and purchase that $400.00 toy for their "knot-head kids"! And I'm just suppose to go without payment but render complete service!

Not in this life, Honey…

True Story:

I once cared for a little girl for about 6 months who was a foster child. Her foster parents, the Bradfords, were going to adopt her. So because she was a "Ward of the State", DCFS was paying 100% of Day Care fees. After she was adopted, DCFS discontinued their payments. She was adopted in the middle of the month and she was cut off in the middle of that month.

I thought it strange that I had not been paid yet. I thought that because she was now adopted, the paperwork slowed up my check so I called DCFS when 2½ months had past and I had not received payment for those 2½ months of service. The Bradfords, who both had very good paying jobs, claimed that they never received notice of the cancellation. I found out later that they just did not want to pay me. DCFS made them comfortable.

DCFS did tell me that in fact their payments had been canceled upon adoption. They were now responsible for all payments. I asked them to look into this matter but they decided that it was too much of an effort. I then told them that it was their responsibility to pay the back fees since DCFS would not. Their total came to almost $900.00. I'd even go along if they were able to pay me $100.00 a month in additional to their regular fees.

Well, that wasn't good enough either. I told them that their daughter could not return until these fees are paid in full. Well, the father got down right ugly. After he received the total bill from me, he called. "Look-a-here. See, a, we all know how these things work, you understand. I'm use to creditors so you don't scare me, you understand. I'm only going to pay you $400.00 and no more, you understand. Otherwise, I can just go through bankruptcy and then you won't get anything! You see what I'm saying?"

I told him that was unacceptable, plus he made me mad! I told him that I wouldn't go any less than $550.00 for my efforts. The sad thing was that he never even intended on paying the $400.00. He just brushed me off as not important. So, I began sending letters. When those didn't work, I solicited the help of a Credit Collections Agency. They go after payments for you. They send out letters and even go as far as to report the "moochers" conduct to the "CREDIT BUREAU" which seriously affects the credit rating of these individuals who won't pay you.

They did go through bankruptcy so I didn't get a thing. However, they shot themselves in the foot for the next eight to ten years, so I feel good about that!

Usually, you only pay them when they collect the money from the other party. It's a percentage, something like 25-30%, give or take. But at least they will collect from them and you'll get more then you would without using this service. Also, they'll pay in more ways than just money for not paying you, *you understand*?!

You are a business, so begin to act like one. Use the aid of a collection agency, you worked for that money, let them go and get it for you.

Chapter 7
The Groceries

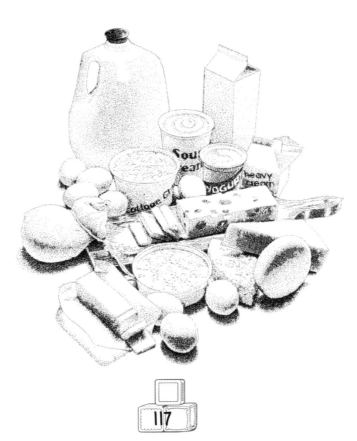

The Groceries

Did you know that there are many providers who are not willing to feed their Day Care children from their own pantry. They would rather the parents bring the food for their children. Well, that makes absolutely no sense to me. Because if you have 8 children, you then have 8 different meals for breakfast, 8 for lunch and 8 for dinner. So in one day you will have prepared 24 different meals for 8 children. Like my girlfriend says, "It ain't that serious!"

There is a program called appropriately, "The Food Program," (check in your area for similar program name), set up by the USDA, (The United States Department of Agriculture). They have provided a way for Child Care facilities to be reimbursed for the food given. Although they have very strict guidelines that must be followed and monitored by it's representatives monthly, it proves to be very beneficial to both the Provider and the children. The Provider receives a check at the end of the month for the food given and the children are guaranteed to receive a well balanced meal.

The purpose for this program is obvious, in this day and time where there are millions of starving and undernourished children all over the world, USDA is striving to eliminate this occurrence within our country by providing this service through our Governmental system. If they can guarantee the funding for the food and the monitoring of the meals within the DCFS affiliations, then every child serviced in this system will not go hungry. Many times, the only meals a child will eat are at the Day Care facility.

Home Day Care Providers can be apart of this program after licensing. After you have received your license in the mail. Be sure and call your local Human Development Center or Child Care Resource and Referral Program and ask for the Food Program carrier in your area. If they have none, ask to be referred to the nearest Program office. The Representative will come to your home and literally spread a TON of paperwork out before you to be read and filled out. It may seem like a lot of information but believe me, you will eventually understand it all.

This is how the Food Program works: USDA may reimburse your for either 2 meals and 1 snack per day per child or 2 snacks and 1 meal per day per child depending on their meal pattern. This pattern is the only pattern acceptable for reimbursement. Your pattern may be a bit different, however, follow it carefully. The Lunch and Dinner meals may cost more in your area than the snacks or breakfast meal so try to put most of your children on your afternoon meals if possible.

Your Representative may give you a stack of Food Program Child Registration Forms and a stack of Menu sheets to be filled out every day for the month. The Registration Forms looks something like the one on the next page. Remember, your forms may look different, this is only an example.

**USDA Food Program Child
Registration Form**

This form must be completed by you
and each mother about their child so
that their child will be counted by the
USDA as being registered with your
Child Care service so that you can be
reimbursed for the money that you've
spent to feed them the approved
meals.

USDA FOOD PROGRAM
CHILD REGISTRATION FORM

To be completed by Home Day Care Provider:

Provider's Name_____ License No._____

Address_____ City_____

****

TO BE COMPLETED BY PARENT OR LEGAL GUARDIAN, PLEASE FILL OUT COMPLETELY

Dear Parent or Legal Guardian:
The Day Care Provider listed above is participating in the Child Care Food Program, a nutrition program
funded by the United States Department of Agriculture(USDA) and sponsored by _____ agency. The
purpose of this program is to promote good eating habits among children. Providers receive cash
reimbursement for approved meals. As a participant, your provider has agreed to follow USDA minimum
standards in the plannng and serving of meals to the children in her/his care. All food served to participating
children must be supplied by the home day care provider.

I certify that the following children are enrolled in the day care home. Usual hours of care will be

_____ to_____, _____
     arrival   departure   days of week
If your home day care provider will be providing care on weekends or holidays on more than an occasional
basis, please explain why:

_____

Is your child(ren) living at the day care providers home? ___yes ___no

Child's first and last name   Child's Age   Child's Birthdate   Is this a Foster
Child

_____
_____
_____

Voluntary Civil Rights Information
Please check the space providing the correct racial and ethnic identity   ___American Indian or Alaskan
of your child(ren). This information is voluntary and will not affect your   ___Asian or Pacific Islands
affect your child's eligibility. This information is being collected only   ___Hispanic
to be sure that everyone receives meals on a fair basis, without regard to   ___Black, not of Hispanic origin
race, color, handicap, sex, age or national origin.   ___While, not of Hispanic origin
   ___Do not wish to give
       information

I hereby certify that the information given on this sheet is true and correct to the best of my knowledge.

_____
Please print Parent/Guardian Name   Home Address   City   Zip

_____
Signature   (Area Code) Home Phone   (Area Code) Work Phone

120

You fill it out, adding each child's name and the time that they are present for that meal. Add up all of the meals served in the appropriate spot and sign and date the form. It may also ask you for your name, address, county, phone number, licensing number and child capacity. Be sure to fill each box out completely so there will be no delay in receiving your check at the end of the month.

Actually, you will receive this months check, for instance, at the end of next month if you turn your form in on time. Each form must be in by the 5th of the next month to receive your check on time by the 30th of that same month. If your form is received after the 5th of the month, it may not go out until the 12th, or whenever their next batch goes out, of that same month which will delay your check until the middle to the end of the next month. So the bottom line is don't be lazy with your paper work. Send it in on time so that if the check is late, it's not your fault, it's the Government's. Of course, your program may be different so be aware that I am only giving you an idea of how this program works.

The Food Program checks, like the Public Aide checks, do come in late sometimes, however, they do come in and are very healthy! Claiming lunch, dinner and 1 snack for 8 children may bring you $450.00 to $500.00 a month, perhaps more in some areas. But whatever the amount, it's worth being on the Program.

One worthwhile benefit that I have found is not only does USDA reimburse me for feeding the Day Care children, but, I am also reimbursed for feeding my own children as well! If your children are under the age of 12 and you meet the financial requirements for the size family that you have minus your Day Care expenses, your children may be included as well if they are eating their meals along with your Day Care children.

The menus are sometimes tricky to fill out, but after you get the hang of what types of food are required, you'll be able to fill them out in your sleep. You must follow the guidelines and have all of the appropriate food components, (cover all the basic good groups like: BREADS AND CEREALS, FRUITS AND VEGETABLES, MEATS AND MEAT ALTERNATIVES, MILK AND DAIRY PRODUCTS), for each meal when filling out the menus, otherwise, you will not get paid for the meal that is missing the right combinations of components at all. And if the children are in your care all day, feed them appropriately all day. However, you will only get paid for the patterns mentioned above. Please don't take the attitude that, "If I'm not getting paid for this meal, I'm not serving it to the kids." You'll have screaming hungry kids on your hands unnecessarily. Just feed them.

True Story:

There was this young girl who was in charge of her 8 younger brothers and sisters while her mother went to work. She loved to watch the TV soaps and at the same time every day, her siblings would scream for lunch. Being that it was rating time, she didn't want to miss the weddings on one show and who killed who on another show so to keep them quiet, she decided to not only give them peanut butter, but she loaded up their sandwiches with it.

She took out from the cabinet the new can of Government issued peanut butter. After opening it, she proceeded to pour out the oil that rests on top. You see, the oil is to be mixed with the peanut meat to make it smooth and creamy enough for consumption! Instead, she drained this Peanut meat of all of it's oil, making it Peanut "Cement"! Then she handed each of her wonderful siblings their "Cement" sandwiches. She thought this would keep them quiet while she enjoyed her shows.

Well, two shows later, she noticed that none of her siblings had returned from the kitchen to annoy her. In fact, except for the television, it was very quiet in the house. As she jumped to her feet, she cried out, "Oh, Lord, I done killed my Mama's kids!!!" She ran into the kitchen only to find each of them carving peanut cement from the roofs of their mouths!

Thought you may enjoy that little true story.

For dinner, you can't just have hot dogs and chips. You must have a meat element, a bread element, 2 vegetables and/or 2 fruits and you MUST have milk. Eliminating any one of these items will result in no MONEY for that meal. The USDA requires that every meal is completely nutritious and covers all of the food group areas.

You may have had three of your four Day Care children all day who have eaten all of your healthy meals and snacks and just before dinner, your fourth child comes in for a couple of hours. His mother fed him junk on her day off all yesterday and throughout the morning. Dinner with you must be a healthy one. Your home is the only place he will receive a really good meal. Every meal must be healthy every day, especially if they are with you 8 to 10 hours every day. It's up to you to not only nurture their little brains but you must feed their little bodies GOOD STUFF for them to grow up healthy and strong. Sometimes you are their "Saving Grace" for the first 3 to 4 years of their little lives; so feed them well.

It may be easier to incorporate your Day Care meals with your family meals. If they all eat the same thing it will be easier on you. So cook larger meals so that everyone will eat the same thing and you won't be so tired and frustrated over cooking two and three dinners in one night.

If it's a spaghetti night, make more spaghetti and feed the Day Care children first to get them out of the way and then feed your family. The same thing with hamburger or fish night.

Learn to work smart and not hard, be wise and thrifty with your shopping. Join a club warehouse so that you can buy in bulk to save on your shopping trips. And shop like you'd shop for your family. The children will learn to like what you like. And likewise, you'll learn how to cook it so that they will eat it.

It may sound like a whole lot to remember but your representative will be available to answer all of your questions, and you *will* have many questions. Just take your time and you'll get the hang of the menu in no time at all.

Your Representative will come to your home periodically to do a surprise menu check. If you haven't been filling out your menus, and here it is the 23rd of the month, there is no way to come up with all of the meals, put in all of the children's names and add up the days while she takes her shoes off and pulls out her paperwork. Don't set yourself up and don't be lazy. Do the menus each month so you can receive your check on time.

Chapter 8
Let's Get Organized

Let's Get Organized

Now that you have all of these papers, forms, contracts, licenses, business papers and children to keep up with, where do you put all of the information so that it won't get lost? You need to put it all in one place where you can put your hands on it when you need it—in a box, plain and simple.

Go to a super store and purchase about 50 basic colorful pocket or file folders, more or less depending on your need, and either a file cabinet or a large heavy duty rubber tub with a lid. I prefer the tub with the lid because it is portable and you can use it to sit on or as a table for the children's activities. When you are done you just wipe clean. Also purchase a pack of stick-on labels.

On each folder, place a sticker in the upper right hand corner and write on them each child's full name. Also include their start date, emergency phone numbers, the parents' SOCIAL SECURITY NUMBER and if they are on Public Assistance, their PUBLIC AID CASE NUMBER. Inside put all of their information, especially their signed contract, registration form, (you'll get a stack of these forms from DCFS), medical record and any other papers you receive on them. **Ask the parents to write out a list of every possible person that might ever pick up their child** and then rewrite this list on the front cover of the folder. Do this with each child and place inside the box.

True Story

This list is very important. About 5 years ago, I cared for a little girl named JaMila whose mother, Tommy, was very young. She was working hard to maintain her independence and keep her apartment. She had to work overtime one particular stormy night and couldn't get to my house by 6:00 p.m. to pick her daughter up so that she wouldn't have to pay the late fee.

She called her Uncle from the city to come into the suburbs and pick up her daughter while she worked late. It was storming really bad. Her Uncle rang the bell and announced to me that he was here to pick up JaMila. I let him in because it was so very miserable outside, but that was wrong judgment on my part. Anyway, he proceeded to tell me that Tommy called him at the last minute to come and get the baby.

He had the names right, and the baby clearly knew him, however, I had never seen him before. There was no record of him on her folder, inside her folder nor under her folder so for all practical purposes, he was a stranger and a potential kidnapper. I told him that I didn't know him and I was very sorry but I just couldn't give this baby to someone I didn't know. I couldn't just take his word for it and give this child to a person not on the mother's list.

I told him that if I were to give him this child and he then turned out not to be who he said he was, first of all I would never forgive myself and secondly, her mother would be out for my head on a silver platter! Well, he was furious! Tommy forgot to call to inform me that she had sent her Uncle to pick up her child. She had just gotten a new job and had not yet given me the phone number and he had no idea where she was working or what her number was.

It was upsetting for him to not only have come through the storm to pick up this child but to be told that he can't take her because Tommy hadn't called me just sent him into "ORBIT!"

In the midst of his screaming and swearing, the phone rang. " Hi, this is Tommy, did my Uncle come to pick up JaMila yet?" She said so sweetly. I handed him the phone. He really gave her "What For," and then handed the phone back to me. I gave him the child and that was that. Tommy and I had a good talk the next day! That list is extremely important.

Anyway, getting back to the labels. You can label the other folders for additional medical record forms, public aide forms, application forms, business account information, license information, food program information and so on.

It's not hard to get organized, it is sometimes hard to stay organized, but make it a routine each Friday to clean up your files and your box. When DCFS comes in to routinely inspect, you'll need to be able to quickly put your hands on specific papers and you don't want to appear that you have no clue of where your important things are. Keep everything in it's place and you'll be prepared when you need your important information in a hurry.

Checklist

❑ This is what I really want to do

❑ Call my local Child Welfare Agency

❑ Filled out the packet completely

❑ Mailed the packet

❑ Have decided to go to classes

❑ Have decided not to go to classes, I will go to the orientation instead

❑ Completed Medical Record forms

❑ Completed Background forms

❑ Fingerprinting done

❑ CPR & Infant First Aid

❑ Mailed off all necessary forms

❑ Pet's inoculations

❑ Call local County Clerk's office

❑ Filled out Assumed Name form

❑ Notary Public has signed all necessary spaces

❑ Mailed out Assumed Name form and fees

❑ Called a local newspaper for publishing

❑ Mailed out the form to the publication

❑ Mailed the published copy back to the Clerk's office

❑ Received Certificate of Ownership of Business

❑ Opened new Business Bank Account

    ❑ Prepared home

    ❑ Prepared kitchen

    ❑ Fire extinguisher

    ❑ Smoke detectors

    ❑ Living Room

    ❑ Dining Room

    ❑ Family Room

    ❑ Basement

❑ First Aid supply kit

❑ Insurance

❏ Day care furniture

    ❏ Beds/cots/cribs

    ❏ Swings

    ❏ Walkers

    ❏ Carriers/car seats

    ❏ Toys

    ❏ Potty chairs

    ❏ Play pens

❏ Sponges/cleaning rags

❏ Bleach solution

❏ Baby wipes/face cloths

❏ Called local Child Welfare Agency for an appointment

❏ Had business cards made up

❏ Had fliers made up

❏ Made copies of fliers

❏ Distributed fliers around town

❏ Worked out rough draft of contract

❏ Finalized contract

❏ Printed out master copy of contract

❏ Made copies of contract

❏ Purchased folders and labels from office supply store

❏ Purchased file cabinet

❏ Received license in the mail

❏ Officially in business as of
_____/_____/_____

I also need:

❏ _____

❏ _____

❏ _____

❏ _____

❏ _____

❏ _____

❏ _____

❏ _____

You will have other things that you will have to follow through on. This is just a list to help you remember the many items that need to be completed.

One Last Thing...

Conclusion

I just want to encourage you to *GO FOR IT*. I believe I've given you enough to get started. In your own city, county or state, you might find that your Home Day Care regulations differ from this book, nevertheless this book is basic common sense *STUFF* that any Home Day Care might follow.

All of the stories within this book are very true. I've changed the names, however, to protect their privacy. You too will be sharing many of your own Home Day Care stories with others, so get your pen and paper out and write some of them down so that you won't forget them.

If you are looking for extra income to supplement your present financial status, yet you need to stay home, Day Care is the perfect alternative. **Just do it**. Don't be afraid of being your own boss. You can do it and do it well. Like you've heard it said, "If I can do it, anybody can", and you can!

Write me soon and let me know how you are doing. And if you have further questions or inquiries, drop me a line or two. My staff and I will do our best to answer your letters.

Send all of your correspondence to me at:

Amber Books
1334 E. Chandler Blvd., Suite 5-D67
Phoenix, AZ 85048

or Call 480-460-1660

I would say good luck to you, but I don't believe in luck. So, I'll just say that I hope you do well and if you know and trust God, He'll direct your path if you let Him. Please remember to be yourself and mold your Day Care, using your own ideas and creativity.

I'll leave you with this; a great Woman in my life once said to me, "Honey, inch by inch and it'll be a cinch!" My beloved Co-Pastor, the Late Pastor Denise M. Turner, gave that to me and I'll give that to you. Take your time and you'll do just fine.

God Bless,

Terri

Appendixes:

Appendix A: You Must Pay Attention

Appendix B: Stress—It's a Killer

Appendix C: They Do Get Sick

Appendix A
You Must Pay Attention

Child Abuse: A Serious Issue

It is estimated that one to two million cases of abuse and/or neglect occur in the U.S. and Canada each year. More than that go undetected. And worse yet, almost four thousand children die every year as a result of inhumane treatment. And many, many more are permanently damaged both physically and mentally as a result of abuse and neglect caused mostly by the ones these babies call mommy and daddy.

Suffering at the hands of a mommy or daddy is a horrible thing for a little one to live through. They have no voice speaking out for their pain. You as the Provider have to be that voice for them. Pay attention to each child coming to you for day care. Get to know the parent and pay attention to what is NOT being said. Many times the parent will tell on themselves by what they don't say or do. Neglect is as important as abuse. What they are not getting is as devastating as the abuse they are getting. So pay attention to the little ones that you are serving and stand up and be that voice for them. You may be the only one that will save their little life.

Once you have become licensed, you are then mandated by your state to report any kind of abuse. While all abuse or neglect is tragic, each case involves a unique and complex set of conditions, like the home environment or financial pressures, individual personalities and temperaments, age, culture differences and religious beliefs, to name a few. It is for these reasons most child abuse laws and definitions are purposely written in its general terms. These terms allow the legal system and social agencies greater flexibility in deciding whether or not a parent has acted irrationally and irresponsibly.

Their ultimate goal usually is to keep the family unit together, wherever possible. If necessary, these agencies will step in and provide safety for the child and counseling for the parent if it means strengthening the home and assuring the child will have a safe, secure environment to grow up to become a functioning and productive adult. Whoever said, "It starts in the home", was right. The good as well as the bad really begins at home. Therefore, your home, which will become the child's second home, must be that voice or that report center for them. If there is anything to tell, they can't tell it, so you must.

When your children come in each day, look at them casually and become familiar with the variations of their different bodies. Now, of course I don't mean strip them each day and have them parade naked before you. I simply mean, just be aware of how they look, become familiar with different bumps and lumps on their neck or arms. Look at their knees and ankles, cheeks and forehead so that if something is different on them, you'll be aware of it.

If you have a child that comes in with scratches on their face, arms and hands every day, it may mean that they have a kitten at home that they play with often and they will get scratches, but if they have scratches that they nor the parents can explain on a daily basis, or they have huge bruises on their face or back, then you'll want to note that. Don't accept "falling down a lot" as an excuse for the many bruises. Something is wrong. You want to write every thought of abuse or neglect down in their folder. Even if it turns out to be nothing, let it be nothing. But if it is something, you have it documented.

You have to allow that "Mother Thing" to kick in. If you feel that something isn't right about that bruise or those scratches, ask the mother about it. Definitely write it down, because if you don't write down what you see and it does turn out to be a situation, if the parent is reported by someone else, like the child's doctor or Sunday School teacher, you can bet your bottom dollar that they WILL blame you. They will swear up and down that they didn't do this thing to their child, but it was the "babysitter" who abused their little darling. Then you will have another situation on your hands.

True Story:

I used to care for these two brothers who were a handful to say the least. There was trouble in the home something awful. You could tell by the way the children responded to authority throughout the day. The younger one was barely 2 and he literally had no concept of interaction with "humans". It was if he spent most of his time at home in the closet! He didn't respond to anything, that is, except a loud voice and his brother's coaching. It was as if he was horribly afraid, so much so that he was frozen in place all day.

The other brother was just a bit older but he grew up much faster. You could quickly tell that he had seen quite a bit. What I mean is, he had been exposed to things a 3-year-old should not be around. While playing, he would act out sexual activity, and because he could speak well his vocabulary was "extensive"!

What do you do with a highly knowledgeable 3-year-old? I kept him by my side all day, as well as his brother. Most of my day was spent in the kitchen while my assistant did activities with the other children. These two brothers could not blend in with the other children at all; so, I kept them with me.

At the end of the first day, I did ask the mother if there was anything I should know concerning her children. She said most assuredly, "No! What do you mean? My kids are fine. What are you talking about...?" Because she quickly got on the defensive, it was obvious there was something there.

I was going to try to work with this mother so the next day rolled around and while changing the younger one's diaper, I noticed these "oozing" little circles on his legs that I didn't notice the day before. I didn't know what these were. They were absolutely disgusting and had puss running from them. I called the mother at work about these circles and she gave me some lame excuse about the children playing in the bushes. In other words, she was aware of these circles but she wasn't going to tell me about them, (strike #1). Then, as I was helping the older child use the potty, I noticed what looked like cigarette burns on his behind and lower back, (strike #2). She had come early to pick them up, so, I asked her about these burns

141

and "*man*", what did I do that for. She got highly upset. She said, "I told you they were playing in the bushes, those ain't no cigarette burns!" She gathered up her children and left in a huff.

I wasn't going to wait for strike #3, I called the abuse hotline in my area and told them all that I had seen. After a day or so, the mother called me fuss'in and cuss'in about how could I do that to her. How could I call DCFS on her and complain about her children being abused. "We was suppose to be 'Sisters-in-the-Lord' and stuff like that", she bellowed. "Huh!", I said to myself. DCFS didn't ask for my name, but she knew it was me because, know one else had been with her children and would have been able to describe with detail what they had seen but me. Apparently, they had come to her house and inspected her children thoroughly.

I told her that if there was nothing there, then she would have nothing to worry about. If she didn't do anything, why then was she so upset. Anyone who calls DCFS for her children, is "for the safety of her children." Well, she never brought them back. I was glad of that.

You have to call when you see something. Let's suppose you don't call and there really is something, you don't want that child to die at the hands of someone you are trying to be friends with. Take the risk of making them mad, it may save that child's life.

There are specific categories of abuse and neglect. They have been identified as:

- ❑ Emotional Neglect
- ❑ Psychological Neglect
- ❑ Physical Neglect
- ❑ Sexual Abuse
- ❑ Emotional Abuse
- ❑ Verbal Abuse
- ❑ Physical Abuse

While I could go on and on about each of these categories, the bottom line is that you as the Provider must be the voice for your children. Pay attention to these babies. Many times the only safe haven is your home. Love them, care for them and protect them. The parents may never thank you for looking out for them, but your heart will know that you did your best.

Appendix B
Stress It's a Killer!

Get Rid Of It!

Plain and Simple, life is not fair. A recent medical study found that continued stress affects ones health tremendously. Those who make an honest effort can begin to rid themselves of this dreaded monster and live longer and happier.

Stress attacks the organs inside your body. The more attacks the weaker they get and eventually something gives out. You must learn how to avoid stress and be determined to maintain peace, both in your home, and in your body, as much as humanly possible.

If you think about it you must have peace at least where you lay your head at night. And if that is not the case, then you might consider having to seek out some professional counseling. Your body needs rest, your mind needs rest, and not only

rest, but peace and quiet. You need that to look forward to so that you don't become a "Nutty Buddy!"

The world needs more good Providers not more good nuts! So here are a few steps to ridding yourself of this killer.

1) **Read the Holy Bible**—God has something special HE wants to share with you. Find out just how much HE really loves you and wants to be a participant in your daily life.

2) **Exercise**—It relieves tension. Take a walk and with each step, imagine that you've stomped on the head of what's stressing you out! Go to the gym and punch it out with gloves, or put the face of that stress monster on the wall and whack at it with racket ball. Dance it out with aerobics, or even jump on a stationary bike and imagine yourself cycling away from it—leaving it in your dust! The list can go on and on. The point is do something to get rid of it.

3) **Make time for healthy friendships**—Get rid of "Dead Buzzard" friends! True friends add to your life and do not take away from it.

4) **Give some of your time to someone who needs to be blessed with your presence**—Spend the day with the person or people you haven't seen in a while but have promised to visit. Take some flowers to Grandma Suzy's house and spend the day with her. Go out to lunch with Aunt Pearl or personally

deliver a "Get Well" card and a bowl of fruit to Uncle Willie. Someone in your life has been asking for a moment of your time, just because they miss you.

5) **Change your diet**—Eat better, eat smarter. In the summer eat more meals but make them lighter and fat-free like salads or raw fruits and veggies. While working with the children during the day, have a bowl of these chopped and peeled raw goodies at arms reach. Better yet, share them with the kiddies. It'll curb your desire to guzzle down fried chicken and biscuits that you've cooked for lunch. You'll have more energy to have more fun with your Day Care children and you'll ultimately become more productive.

6) **Take time/Make time for YOU**—Schedule time for a bath! Sit quietly and soak in a hot tub of soothing bubbles, sweetly scented oil in the water, candles and soft music. Here is a simple easy to make bath tonic that you can put together from your own kitchen.

Save a cute squeeze bottle and fill it with more or less of these ingredients depending on your personal desires:

❑ Light pure vegetable oil (For your skin)

❑ Baby shampoo or Baby bath (For the bubbles). You can use any kind of liquid soap as long as it doesn't have strong grease-fighting agents in it.

❏ Any extract you prefer like, Vanilla, Almond or Peppermint (For a calming relaxing scent)

❏ Honey (It softens your skin, especially your feet.)

❏ A few drops of blue or green food coloring (it makes everything look pretty!)

Now shake that bottle up and squeeze it out under the running water. It smells so good and the heated oil and honey sinks right into your skin for a smooth soft finish to a lovely bath. No one can be you but you; so take time to get to know YOU.

7) **Plan your day better**—Schedule everything even a nap. If you write out your day, you'll have things to look forward to. You'll get things done and your day won't schedule you.

8) **Look for the humor in every situation**—things won't always go smoothly. They may not even go your way. The best of plans fall apart sometimes. If you must cry about it, do so. Afterwards, look at it for what it really is…a learning experience. Laugh at it, and then go on. You'll never go from level to level if you get stuck and break down on every turn. You might get stuck but don't stay stuck!

9) **Confide in the LORD about your troubles**—HIS date book always has open appointments for counseling. HIS services are free because all of your time has been paid by an admirer—Jesus Christ.

10) **Consciously avoid "Toxic Persons" in your life**—These people definitely take away from your life and seriously violate your personal space. Run as far away from them as possible and then get on the nearest bus or train and go farther! Do whatever it takes to keep these people out of your life. Constant conflict and agitation only brings about stress; and too much stress will end your life prematurely. You have too much to do…Toxic Persons will make your busy life impossible to live.

11) **Attend ONE church and be consistent**—Good Godly fellowship is important as well as necessary for the inner-man. Each church serves a different doctrine or meal; and eating from assorted tables may make you sick, not to mention confused. God honors faithfulness. Be faithful to one church. Nothing can grow well if it doesn't have a chance to take root!

12) **Go outside and play at least once a week**—Even if you lay out under a tree, the fresh air clears the head of indoor stuffiness. Change your scenery. Go to a movie, the mall or just a drive around town. You'll be surprised at how much more sharper your vision will be for your Day Care, if you take time to look at something else. Do this WITHOUT the children!

13) **Learn to enjoy saying "No"**—Sometimes people, places and things will change your schedule. While at times, it may be okay to stray from your set agenda for a moment. Getting into the habit of allowing these distractions to alter your day, causes you to feel out of control. Again your day is over and your children have

done nothing. Stress and frustration will begin to set in when all you have to do is say one little word. When you really look at it, "<u>*NO*</u>" is a pretty enjoyable little statement!

14) **Lose yourself in your other desires**—The time you've set aside for yourself should be spent on doing something else other than Day Care. Really get into that book, or try out that new recipe, or pull out that canvas and those paints, etc....Lose yourself for a minute, or two, or three...It's really okay to do so!

I once saw a great note left on the desk of a busy man who went out to play:

> *I'm not here,*
> *I've gone to find myself.*
> *If I return before I get back,*
> *Please keep me here until I return!*

Get a daily planner or at least a notebook and write everything out that you've got to do for the day. Plan everything, even rest and recreation. Your days with your children will go a lot smoother and you'll find that no one will be able to dictate to you what to do with your time. After all, if time is money, you don't want anyone wasting your precious commodity.

Appendix C
They Do Get Sick

Plain and simple. Children all get sick at some point in time. When you have a new parent, be conscious of the fact that new parents especially, "freak out" when their brand new darling comes down with an illness. They will act as if their baby will never recover.

True Story:

I had a mother once who left my house rushing to the emergency room because little Johnny had the sniffles and she didn't know what to do. His little nose was running just a tiny bit and she was losing it. I didn't know at the time that she was headed for the emergency room. She called me after having been seen by the Doctor saying that she was staying home for the rest of the week to make sure that he would be fine. Even though the Doctor said that he was perfectly healthy, she wanted to make sure. "You know they could be wrong," she said with a trembling voice.

Children have to develop an immunity to your house, especially if you have a pet. They are around new children and a new environment so sniffles are expected. And in the winter time, they are going to get colds and coughs.

Germs are every where, especially in a day care setting. The children are always putting things in their mouths, they are coughing on each other or sneaking a drink from each other's cup and so on. As much as you try to keep things clean, a germ or two will get past you and into their little systems. It is to be expected.

If a child does come down with an illness, in your contract you will note that the ill child MUST remain at home until he/she recovers. It is not fair for the parent to expect you to care for their sick child. You do not have the time to cater to a sick child. They have to make arrangements to have the child cared for while they are ill, especially if it is a communicable illness.

What will they do after you catch their child's illness, they certainly have to find alternate care then, you are sick!

You will find many times over that parents will bring their darling to you and run back out to work and they know that their child is SICK, SICK, SICK. Now, you have to deal with this sick child until you can reach the parent at work. And they know it so they conveniently are not at their desk or are on the phone…all day. While, they may not really notice that they are infecting the other children and you with their child's illness, they would be ready to kill if another child infects their child with that same illness.

Hold firm and stand your ground and tell that parent little Kianna can't return until that illness is completely gone. If necessary require a Doctor's note assuring their total recovery. Something like "ringworm" can go around and around forever if you allow that infected child to continue to stay in your care with nothing more than a bandage covering that affected area. A thing like ringworm is in their system and under their finger nails. It takes medication to kill that fungus, don't let a mother tell you that she's been putting "bleach" on it so it's okay.

True Story:

I thought I was in desperate need of children once so I was willing to take any amount of pay. I had a mother who couldn't pay much but needed someone to watch her son for the summer during the day while she was at work. I figured, well, he's older, he can run around outside with my kids. She could only afford something like $30.00 a week for 8 hours a day, Monday through Friday. I was so in need of money that I was going to accept that.

We were sitting at my kitchen table getting ready to sign the contract and her son runs in and interrupts our little meeting. "Ma, Ma", he says in a panic, "This bandage keeps coming off and this thing itches real bad." And he proceeds to scratch as he'd been doing for some time. It was very red and obviously inflamed. I asked her what was that on his chin. She said in a matter-of-fact tone, "Oh, chil' this thing keeps coming back. This time it's on his chin. I keep putt'in bleach on it and it goes away but then, it shows up somewhere else. He always git this thing. Someone said it was that ringworm thang, but chil' I don't know what it is. I ain't going to no

Doctor, cause I cain't pay no bill. I ain't got no 'Ensurance' so bleach'll have to do! " Then she turns to her son, "Boy, quit scratch'in it, go back out an play, I'll be done in a minute!"

Right there shows the insensitivity and irresponsibility of a parent. Whoever he is playing with will become infected with the "ringworm thang". I quickly said to her that if that is ringworm, it is highly contagious; and her son is giving it to any child he plays with. I couldn't have him in my home unless that was completely gone and I had a note from the Doctor stating that he, in fact, has been treated and the illness is completely gone. Well, she didn't want to hear any part of what I had to say so she got mad and left. A few days later, she was evicted from her home and left the neighborhood. No amount of money would have been worth that.

That bleach sounds crazy but it's true. Parents, you'll find, have their own way of handling very contagious illnesses and you have to nip it in the bud when it comes to bringing it into your home. Above all else, this is where you live and sleep, you can't have some disease lurking around in your carpeting, on your couch and so on. You can't have it and you won't have it. If it means that mom or dad must take off work, make a trip to a Doctor, or find alternate care, then so be it. Your rules are your rules, no amount of money is worth getting sick over.

I have gathered a list of common communicable diseases that you should watch out for. Make yourself somewhat familiar with them and do whatever is necessary to control the outbreak of these diseases in your home.

Communicable Illness	Signs and Symptoms	Infectious Agent	Methods of Transmission	Incubation Period	Length of Communicability	Control Measures
Acquired Immune Deficiency Syndrome	Flu-like symptoms, including fatigue, weight loss, enlarged lymph glands persistent cough, fever and diarrhea	Virus	Children acquire virus when born to infected mothers, from breast milk of infected mothers and from contaminated blood transfusions. Adults acquire the virus via sexual transmission, contaminated drug needles and blood transfusions.	6 weeks to 8 years	A lifetime	Exclude children 0-5 years if they have open lesions, uncontrollable nosebleeds, bloody diarrhea, or are at high risk for exposing others to blood-contaminated body fluids. Wear disposable gloves to clean up body fluids; use good hand washing techniques. Seal contaminated items, like diapers, tissues or paper towels in plastic bags. Disinfect surfaces with chlorine solution, (1 part bleach:10 parts water) or other disinfectant.
Chickenpox	Slight fever, irritability, cold-like symptoms. Red rash which develops blister-like head, scabs later. Most abundant on covered parts of the body like chest, stomach, back neck or forearms.	Virus	Airborne through contact with secretions from the respiratory tract. Transmission from contact with blisters not common.	2 to 3 weeks after exposure	2 to 3 days prior to the onset of symptoms until 5 or 6 days after first eruptions. Scabs are not contagious.	Specific control measures like A.) Exclusion of sick child B.) Practice good personal hygiene, especially careful hand washing. Children can return to the Day Care when all blisters have formed a dry scab which is about 1 week.
Cold Sore or Fever Blister	Clear blisters usually on the face and lips which crust and heal within a few days.	Virus	Direct contact with saliva of infected person	Up to 2 weeks	Virus remains in saliva for as long as 7 weeks following recovery.	No specific control. Good personal hygiene. Child does not have to be excluded from the group.

Communicable Illness	Signs and Symptoms	Infectious Agent	Methods of Transmission	Incubation Period	Length of Communicability	Control Measures
Conjunctivitis or Pinkeye	Redness of the white portion of the eye and inner aspects of the lids. Swelling of the lids and a yellow discharge from the eyes.	Bacteria or Virus	Direct contact with discharge from eyes or upper respiratory tract of an infected person. Also through contaminated fingers and objects like tissues or towels.	1 to 3 days	Throughout active infection, several days up to 2 to 3 weeks.	Antibiotic treatment. Exclude child from care until eyes have been treated and there is no discharge or the Doctor can provide a sufficient note. Strict personal hygiene and careful hand washing.
Common Cold	Highly contagious infection of the upper respiratory tract accompanied by slight fever, chills, runny nose, fatigue and muscle aches and pains.	Virus	Airborne through contact with secretions from the respiratory tract like coughs, sneezing, eating utensils and the like.	12 to 72 hours	About 1 day before onset of symptoms to 2 to 3 days after acute illness	Prevention through education and good personal hygiene. Avoid exposure. Exclude the child for the first two days. Antibiotics are not effective against this virus. Avoid aspirin products. Watch for complications such as earaches, bronchitis, croup or pneumonia.
Dysentery	Sudden onset of vomiting, diarrhea. May be accompanied by high fever and/ or headache or abdominal pain. Stools may contain blood, pus or mucus. Can be fatal in young children	Bacteria	Rectal-oral transmission by contaminated objects or indirectly through ingestion contaminated food or water.	1 to 7 days	May last up to 4 weeks or longer	Careful handwashing after bowel movement or diaper changes. Proper disposal of human feces. Control of flies and strict adherence to sanitary procedures for food preparation.
Encephalitis	Sudden onset of headache, high fever, convulsions, vomiting, confusion, neck and back stiffness, tremors and coma.	Virus	Indirect spread by bites from disease-carrying mosquitoes. Also by tick bites in some areas.	5 to 15 days	Humans are not contagious	Spraying of mosquito breeding areas and use of insect repellents as well as public education.

Communicable Illness	Signs and Symptoms	Infectious Agent	Methods of Transmission	Incubation Period	Length of Communicability	Control Measures
Giardiasis	An intestinal parasite infection of the small bowel. Typical symptoms include chronic diarrhea, abdominal cramping, bloating, pale and foul-smelling stools, weight loss, and fatigue.	Parasite	Rectal-oral transmission, through contact with infected stool like diaper changes, or soiled underwear, poor hand washing or contaminated toy to mouth. Also transmitted trough contaminated water sources.	1 to 4 days	As long as the parasite is present in the stool.	Infected persons must be treated with medication. Strictest handwashing discipline before eating or preparing food and after using the bathroom. Good sanitary conditions maintained in bathroom areas.
Haemophilus Influenza Type B	An acute respiratory infection frequently causes meningitis. Other complications include pneumonia and arthritis, infections of the bloodstream and conjunctivitis.	Bacteria	Airborne by secretions of the respiratory tract such as nose or throat. Persons can also be carriers with or without symptoms.	2 to 4 days	Throughout acute phase, as long as organism is present. Non-communicable 36 to 48 hours after treatment with antibiotics.	Identify and remove such children. Treat the medication 3 to 4 days before returning to day care. Notify parents of exposure and urge parents to contact their physician. Immunize children. Practice good handwashing techniques; sanitize contaminated objects.
Hepatitis Infectious Type A	Fever, fatigue, loss of appetite, nausea, abdominal pain in the liver area. Illness may be accompanied by yellowing of the skin and eyeballs, (jaundice) in adults, but not always in children.	Virus	Rectal-oral transmission. Also spread by contaminated food, water, milk and objects like toys.	10 to 50 days with an average length of 30 to 35 days	7 to 10 days prior to onset of symptoms to not more than 7 days after onset of jaundice.	Exclude from day care a minimum of 2 weeks following onset. Special attention to careful handwashing after going to the bathroom and before eating is critical following an outbreak. Report disease incidences to public health authorities.

Communicable Illness	Signs and Symptoms	Infectious Agent	Methods of Transmission	Incubation Period	Length of Communicability	Control Measures
Impetigo	Infection of the skin forming a crusty, moist lesion usually on the face, ears and around the nose. Highly contagious. Common among children.	Bacterial	Direct contact with discharge from sores indirect contact with contaminated articles of clothing, tissues, etc.	2 to 5 days. May be as long as 10 days.	Until lesions are healed.	Exclusion from day care until lesions have been treated with antibiotics for 24 to 48 hours.
Lice of the Head	Lice are seldom visible to the naked eye. White nits or eggs may be apparent on the hair shafts. The most obvious symptom is itching of the scalp, especially behind the ears and at the base of the neck.	Head louse	Direct contact with infected persons or with their personal articles like hats hair brush, combs or clothing. Lice can survive for 2 to 3 weeks on pillows, bedding, carpets, furniture and car seats.	Nits hatch in 1 week and reach maturity within 2 weeks.	While lice remain alive on infested persons or clothing. Until nits have been destroyed.	Infested children should be excluded from day care until treated. Hair should be washed with a special medication and rinsed with vinegar/water solution to ease removal of all nits using a fine-tooth comb. Heat from a hair dryer also helps destroy the eggs. All friends and family and day care children should be checked. Thoroughly clean child's environment totally and seal nonwashable items in plastic bag for one month.
Measles (Rubeola)	Fever, cough, runny nose, eyes sensitive to light. Dark red blotchy rash that often begins on the face and neck, then spreads over the entire body. Highly communicable.	Virus	Airborne through coughs, sneezes and contact with contaminated articles.	8 to 13 days. A rash develops approximately 14 days after exposure.	From beginning of symptoms until 4 days after rash appears.	Most effective control method is immunization. Good personal hygiene, especially handwashing and covering coughs. Exclude child from day care for at least 4 days after rash appears.

Communicable Illness	Signs and Symptoms	Infectious Agent	Methods of Transmission	Incubation Period	Length of Communicability	Control Measures
Mononucleosis	Characteristic symptoms include sore throat, intermittent fever, fatigue, and enlarge lymph glands in the neck. May also be accompanied by headache and enlarged liver or spleen.	Virus	Airborne. Also direct contact with the mouth of an infected person.	10 to 14 days for children and 30 to 50 days for adults.	Unknown. Organisms may be present in oral secretions for as long as one year following illness.	None known. Child should be kept home until the acute phase is over, usually 6 to 10 days.
Mumps	Sudden onset of fever with swelling of the salivary glands.	Virus	Airborne through coughing or sneezing. Also direct contact with oral secretions of infected persons.	12 to 26 days.	4 to 6 days prior to the onset of symptoms until swelling in the salivary glands is gone, usually 7 to 9 days.	Immunization provides permanent protection. Peak incidence is in winter and spring. Exclude child from day care until all symptoms have disappeared.
Pinworms	Irritability and itching of the rectal area. Common among young children	Parasite. Not contagious from animals	Infectious eggs are transferred from person to person by contaminated hands, oral-rectal transmission. Indirectly spread by contaminated bedding, food, clothing, swimming pools and other public areas.	Life cycle of the worm is 3 to 6 weeks. A person can re-infect themselves.	2 to 8 weeks or as long as a source of infections remains present.	Infected children must be excluded from day care until treated with medication. After which they may return after initial dose. All infected and non-infected members of a family must be treated as one time. Frequent handwashing is essential. Discourage nail biting or sucking on fingers. Daily baths and change of linen are necessary. Disinfect toilet seats at least once a day. Vacuum carpeted areas daily. Eggs are also destroyed when exposed to temperatures over 132 F. Education and good personal hygiene are vital to controlling this illness.

Communicable Illness	Signs and Symptoms	Infectious Agent	Methods of Transmission	Incubation Period	Length of Communicability	Control Measures
Ringworms	An infection of the scalp, skin or nails. Causes flat, spreading oval-shaped lesions that may become dry and scaly or moist and crusty. When it is present on the feet it is commonly called athlete's foot. Infected nails may become discolored, brittle or chalky or they may disintegrate.	Fungus	Direct or indirect contact with infected persons, their personal items showers, swimming, pools theater seats, etc. Dogs and cats may also be infected and transmit it to children or adults	1 to 4 days. Unknown for athlete's foot.	As long as lesions are present.	Exclude children from day care where they are likely to expose others. May return to day care following medical treatment with a fungicidal ointment. Affected area must be flat and all trace of crusts or scales or scabs must be completely gone before the child may return. All shared areas should be thoroughly cleansed with a fungicide.
Rocky Mountain Spotted Fever	Onset usually abrupt fever about 101 to 104F. Joint pain, severe nausea and vomiting and white coating on the tongue. Rash appears on the 2nd to the 5th day over forehead, wrist and ankles. Later it covers the entire body. Can be fatal if not treated.	Bacteria	Indirect transmission, tick bite.	2 to 14 day with an average length of 7 days.	Not contagious from person to person.	Prompt removal of ticks, not all ticks cause illness. Administration of antibiotics. Use insect repellent on clothes when outdoors.
Roseola Infantum 6 mo. To 3 yrs.	Most common in the spring and fall. Fever rises abruptly 102 to 105F and lasts 3 to 4 days. Loss of appetite, listlessness, development of rash on trunk, arms and neck lasting 1 to 2 days.	Virus	Unknown	10 to 15 days	1 to 2 days before onset to several days following fading of the rash.	Exclude from day care during acute phase.

Communicable Illness	Signs and Symptoms	Infectious Agent	Methods of Transmission	Incubation Period	Length of Communicability	Control Measures
Rubella (German measles)	Mild fever. Rash begins on the face and neck and rarely lasts more than 3 days. May have an arthritis-like discomfort and swelling in joints.	Virus	Airborne through contact with respiratory secretions like coughing and sneezing.	14 to 21 days	From one week prior to 5 days following onset of the rash.	Immunization offers permanent protection. Children must be excluded from day care for at least 5 days.
Salmonellosis	Abdominal pain and cramping, sudden fever, sever diarrhea which may contain blood, nausea and vomiting lasting 5 to 7 days.	Bacteria	Rectal-oral transmission by dirty hands. Also contaminated food, improperly cooked poultry, milk, eggs, and infected animals.	6 to 48 hours	Throughout acute illness. May remain o carrier for months.	Attempt to identify source. Exclude from day care until symptoms end. Carrier should not handle or prepare food until stool cultures are negative. Practice good hand washing and sanitizing procedures.
Scabies	Characteristic tunnels under the skin, especially between the fingers and around the wrists, elbows, waist, thighs and buttocks. Causes intense itching.	Parasite	Direct contact with an infected person.	Several days to 4 weeks	Until all mites and eggs are destroyed.	Children should be excluded from day care until treated. Affected persons should bathe with prescribed soap and carefully launder all bedding and clothing. All contacts of infected persons must be notified.
Streptococcal Infections - Strep throat Scarlatina Rheumatic fever	Sudden. High fever accompanied by sour, red throat. May also have nausea, vomiting, headaches, white patches on tonsils and enlarged glands. Development of a rash depends on the infectious organism.	Bacteria	Airborne by droplets from coughs or sneezes. May also be transmitted by food and raw milk.	1 to 4 days	Throughout the illness and for approximately 10 days afterward unless treated eliminated communicability within 36 hours. Can develop rheumatic fever or become a carrier if not treated.	Exclude child from day care with symptoms. Antibiotic treatment is essential.

Communicable Illness	Signs and Symptoms	Infectious Agent	Methods of Transmission	Incubation Period	Length of Communicability	Control Measures
Tetanus	Muscular spasm and stiffness especially around the neck and mouth. Can lead to convulsions and inability to breathe and death.	Bacteria	Indirect. Enter the body through wounds and unnoticed cuts. Organisms live in the soil and dust.	4 days to 2 weeks	Not contagious	Immunization every 8 to 10 years gives complete protection.

Illness is a very common occurrence when you have children. You as the Provider must try your best to control the outbreak of these different diseases whenever possible. Some things you really just cannot help. All I ask, all the Parents really ask and all of the children you will ever serve are just asking you to protect them, care well for them and do your very best to help keep them healthy and happy for as long as you are serving them.

When My Day Care Baby Went Home

You know, time is a funny thing. It has no favoritism. It is cruel and constant. Everyone has only one measure of it. Some have as much as 80 or 90 years of it while yet others only get as little as 16 months of it.

This was the hardest thing that I have ever done. Hold a mother in my arms because her baby, my Day Care baby, is dead.

Make no mistake about it, these children who come into your home become a part of your life. They become a part of your family. You are the one raising them. Feeding and caring for them. Rocking them to sleep, teaching them and training them. And when they are gone, it's hard. What do you say? Nothing, just be there.

We got a call in the middle of the night to come quickly, Christopher has been in an accident. His mother, Rene, was delirious with grief. Her baby boy, her only child, was killed. What could we say, what could we do.

My husband spoke to the family first. He then prayed for her as she was in immeasurable pain and crying hysterically. Then he left the room. I was alone with her. She asked me, begged me to go and get him. "You have to go and get him, he's crying.

163

He'll come to you, please go and get him for me, please!" Everything in me wanted to go and bring him back to her. I told her to rest. "He's fine. He's asleep so you rest."

I left the room and went to where my husband was. We spoke with the family for a moment and then we went on home. We sat on the couch together and cried till morning.

I visited her every day for the next 5 or 6 days. She was in no shape to take care of the necessities so her Mother asked me to stay and keep an eye on her.

She wanted me to help her with the obituary and selecting appropriate pictures. She was so hurt. What could I say to her that would mean anything? She still carried the diaper bag, jacket and blanket that was around him at the time of the accident.

One moment he was here, and the next moment, he was gone. He was sitting in the front, in her lap and in an instant he was with the Lord!

I thought I could hold it together as I read his obituary to the audience during the funeral, but I couldn't. I cried as I told her, "While he can never come back to you, you can surely go to him. Live a full life so that you'll have lots to tell him when you get there." And then I took my seat.

She came to see me weeks later to say Thank You. Not for helping out in his death, but helping out in his life. He was really a special child.

I run into her occasionally in the shopping center that I frequent. She's doing fine. One day, while I was in the store, I saw her and our eyes met from across the room. She gave me a wink and a nod.

She came to visit me the other day. It was the first time she'd been back since Christopher's death. We sat at the table and had small talk. With tears in her eyes, she turned and thanked me again. And then she announced that Christopher was going to be a "Heavenly Big Brother"!

I screamed with great joy for her. I laughed and cried at the same time as I hugged her tight.

I do believe she's going on with her life so that she'll have lots to tell him when she gets there.

I've begun an annual summer Family Picnic in honor of my Day Care child, Christopher.

> *My love to all of you, and good luck.*
> *Terri*

Terri Simmons, Ph.D., is a fiercely religious woman who puts God above all. Married to Michael Simmons for 19 years, she is also the mother of five children: Michael Jr., 14; Marcus, 12; Matthew, 10; Mitchell, 8; and Taylor, 3. Terri also lectures, gives motivational seminars and is an instructor at several colleges teaching home day care and has also attained her doctorate in early childhood education.

ORDER FORM

Fax Orders: 480-283-0991   Postal Orders: Send Checks and Money Orders to:
Telephone Orders: 480-460-1660   **Amber Books Publishing**
Online Orders: E-mail: Amberbk@aol.com   **1334 East Chandler Blvd., Suite 5-D67**
                                                Phoenix, AZ 85048

Please send _____ copy/ies of *How to Own and Operate Your Home Day Care Business Successfully Without Going Nuts!* by Dr. Terri Simmons.

Please send _____ copy/ies of *The African-American Woman's Guide to Successful Make-up and Skin Care* by Alfred Fornay.

Please send _____ copy/ies of *How to Play the Sports Recruiting Game and Get an Athletic Scholarship: The Handbook and Guide to Success for the African-American High School Student-Athlete* by Rodney J. McKissic.

Please send _____ copy/ies of *Is Modeling for You? The Handbook and Guide for the Young Aspiring Black Model* by Yvonne Rose and Tony Rose.

Name:_____

Company Name:_____

Address:_____

City:_____State:____Zip:_____

Telephone: (_____) _____

For Bulk Rates Call: **480-460-1660**

ORDER NOW

Home Day Care	$12.95
Successful Make-up	$14.95
Sports Recruiting:	$12.95
Modeling:	$14.95

❑ Check ❑ Money Order ❑ Cashiers Check

Payable to: Amber Books
1334 E. Chandler Blvd., Suite 5-D67
Phoenix, AZ 85048

Shipping: $5.00 per book.
Allow 7 days for delivery.

Sales Tax: Add 7.05% to books shipped to
Arizona addresses.

Total enclosed: $_____